Salford
— IN THE DAYS OF —
STEAM

Paul Shackcloth

One of Bolton's stud of Stanier Class 4 2-6-4 tank engines, No 42656 rattles over New Bailey Street bridge and into the platforms at Salford Station. The train is the 5.45pm from Manchester Victoria to Bolton Trinity Street, calling at all stations, and is due to arrive at 6.13pm. **11th JULY 1957** ● **K. FIELD**

PAUL SHACKCLOTH

Salford
IN THE DAYS OF
STEAM

First published 2004

ISBN 0 9543128 2 1

Published by Steam Image, PO Box 90, Cheadle Hulme, Cheshire SK8 6WZ and printed by Deanprint Ltd, Stockport, Cheshire SK3 0PR.

FOREWORD

The City of Salford is often referred to in railway circles only in a historical context. It has, of course, been well documented that it played a major part in the development of the *Liverpool and Manchester Railway* but, by way of contrast, the early incursions by both the Lancashire and Yorkshire and the London and North Western Railway companies into the area seem scant. This volume, hopefully, goes a small way to redressing the balance. Over the years, Salford has always suffered from living in the shadow of its more illustrious neighbour Manchester. Although of city status, it has no focal point and the town hall, which is situated in Bexley Square off Chapel Street - the main thoroughfare, hardly compares with the Manchester equivalent. This lack of national identity wasn't helped by the LNWR, whose principal station in the area was named Manchester Exchange in 1884, yet lay within the Salford boundary. Similarly the racecourse and much of the dockland area, well within its borders, were called Manchester.

The city, nevertheless, had many proud traditions and was rich in industrial heritage. One example, which becomes evident in this book, is the Corporation's bus fleet, which throughout the 1950's and early 1960's, set such high standards that it became the envy of the vast majority of other municipal operators.

I have once more deliberately created a similar balance within the boundary after the districts of Eccles, Irlam, Swinton and Pendlebury and Worsley had been absorbed. The scope extends further to Walkden and Ellenbrook in the west and Whitefield in the north, but concentrates on Manchester Exchange Station and the Motive Power Depots at Agecroft and Patricroft. The vast majority of the 450+ photographs are individually credited but inevitably some remain anonymous. As with my previous books, I have acknowledged the collector in these instances, but wish to apologise in advance if any have 'slipped through the net'.

A work such as this would have been impossible without the help of a great number of people. Prominent individuals who have given freely of their time in offering information, advice and, in some cases, access to their own collections include: Jim Carter, Gordon Coltas, Fred Consterdine, Bernard Crick, Alan Gilbert, Brian Green, Richard Greenwood, John Hartshorne, Trevor Moseley, John Ryan and Allan Sommerfield.

My thanks are once again extended to Peter Thompson for providing a selection of views of the major bus operators, many of whose buses are seen at work, and also to Ted Gray - whose knowledge of the Salford Transport scene is legendary, for further assistance.

ACKNOWLEDGEMENTS

Jean Milton at the *Manchester Museum of Science and Industry*, Paula Moorhouse at the *Manchester Central Local Studies Library*, David Postle and Ian Cockcroft at the *Kidderminster Railway Museum* and Tim Ashworth, Head Librarian at the *Salford Local History Library* all deserve recognition, having contributed in one way or another.

The images credited to Kenneth Field, Tom Lewis, Eric Bentley and Jim Davenport appear courtesy of Rail Archive Stephenson, *The Manchester Locomotive Society* and Norman Preedy, Jean Bentley and Brian Green respectively. Additional material has been supplied by Graham Whitehead, Peter Fitton, Derek Shepherd, Richard Casserley, Ken Fairey, Paul Jordan, Mike Bentley, Brian Cramer, Tony Renshaw, Peter Michie, Dave Jessop, Bob Miller, Ron Simpson, Roger Carpenter, Ted Hancock, Peter Hutchinson, Paul Bolger, Jeremy Suter, Joe Leighton, Tom Heavyside, Ken Nuttall, Robert Humm, Dave Hampson, John Fozard, Steve Leyland, Eric Humphrey, Neville Knight, David Pass, Noel Machell, Bert Pilkington, Peter Groom, George Bingham and members of the *Manchester Locomotive Society*. If I have inadvertently missed anyone, please accept my apologies.

Once again, David Young and Arthur Haynes have proved to be tireless workers in the project whilst my wife Norma, who has tolerantly suffered further inconvenience, continues to add her support. To all, I offer a very sincere 'thank you'.

AUGUST 2004 ● **PAUL SHACKCLOTH**

DEDICATION

I wish to dedicate this book to another member of my family - Arthur Haynes. He has always been an avid railway enthusiast whose interests also extend to both the modelling and bus scenes. Such enthusiasm was bound to rub off on his nephew, especially after he presented him with his first ABC Combined Volume as a Christmas present in 1957. The significance of spotting a York V2, No 60848 on Gorton shed whilst accompanying him one Sunday morning as a 'junior gricer' on a local RCTS trip was lost at the time, but one which I appreciated many years later.

In addition, I wish to couple this dedication to the memory of the late Wilf Cooper - a fellow enthusiast and prolific photographer whose splendid railway images of the Salford area did so much to preserve the city's posterity.

MANCHESTER EXCHANGE STATION - CATHEDRAL APPROACH

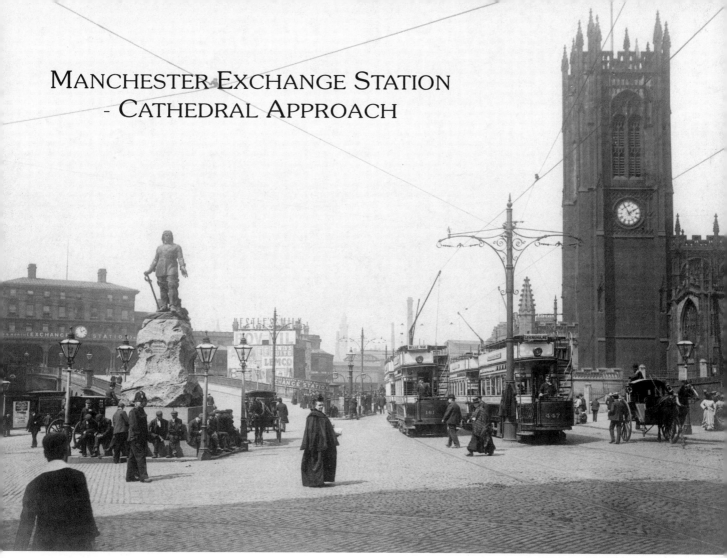

The Edwardian elegance of Manchester is reflected in this familiar view of Victoria Street, the station approach and its environs. Behind the photographer stood the triangular shaped Victoria Buildings bounded by Deansgate, St. Mary's Gate and Victoria Street with the 170 bedroom Victoria Hotel overlooking this scene. These buildings were totally destroyed by enemy action in December 1940. The Oliver Cromwell memorial statue, sculpted by Matthew Noble, was presented to the city in 1875 by Mrs Abel Heywood in memory of her husband. Sat around its base are any number of men, who could always be found on a nice day watching the world go by. A new home was located in Wythenshawe Park in 1968 when the statue's position hindered major road development. Occupying part of the land which was later to become Salford Bus Station was the travel agency of Thomas Cook and Son. Established in 1840, the firm were closely associated with excursion trains in the early days of rail travel. During the Edwardian era, clocks were in unison with each other - the one of four on the tower of Manchester Cathedral and that fronting Manchester Exchange Station both showing 1.55pm. At least four open-top Manchester Corporation trams are in view, the leading two of which are discernable. No **161** was one of the first build of 4-wheel electric trams delivered by Brush in 1901/2. No 173 of this batch has been restored to its original condition after serving as a garden shed for many years. The Victoria Street - Belle Vue service began operation on 1st June 1902 and in 1914 became Service 14. Between 1926 and 1937 the route was extended to Weaste and so became a jointly operated cross-city service. No **447** was a bogie open-top car, also built by Brush in 1901/2. In 1923 it was totally enclosed and fitted with new bogies as part of a general rebuilding programme. The Victoria Street to Levenshulme tram began running on 2nd August 1904, becoming Service 36 in 1914. From 1926 it became Service 37 leaving No 36 to represent another cross-city service - the Levenshulme to Kersal route.   **1909** ● **SALFORD LOCAL HISTORY LIBRARY**

Something appears to have caught the attention of the ice cream seller and his street trading colleague. The incident has certainly distracted them away from the photographer and the result is this wonderful candid scene. The three young boys are oblivious to anything other than the ice cream anyway, one having climbed on to the axle to inspect the contents of the tub. Two more are slumped on the pavement whilst another appears to have lost the contents of his pockets. Behind them is a hoarding advertising destinations served by Exchange Station. The LNWR offered a *direct* route to Liverpool in a bid to entice passengers away from the L&Y and CLC. Also featured are Ireland, Wigan, Preston, the English Lakes and all stations to Scotland. Meanwhile a licensed horse drawn cab slowly makes its way up the approach road. Fares and conditions were regulated by the local authority but the public had the choice of either hiring by the hour or by the distance travelled, depending on the number of people sharing.   **1909** ● **SALFORD LOCAL HISTORY LIBRARY**

CONTENTS

Manchester Exchange Station 5

Manchester Victoria Station 25

The Gateway to Salford 31

Salford Station 39

Irwell Street Goods Station 46

L&Y Salford Docks Branch 52

Windsor Bridge - Brindle Heath 53

Agecroft MPD 65

Pendleton - Walkden High Level 77

Pendleton (Old) - Kearsley 86

Heaton Park - Whitefield 92

Passing Salford Station 94

Ordsall Lane 96

Cross Lane - Eccles 102

Eccles Station - Barton Moss Junction 109

Patricroft MPD 125

The Monton Line 147

City of Salford 159

SALFORD AND DISTRICT

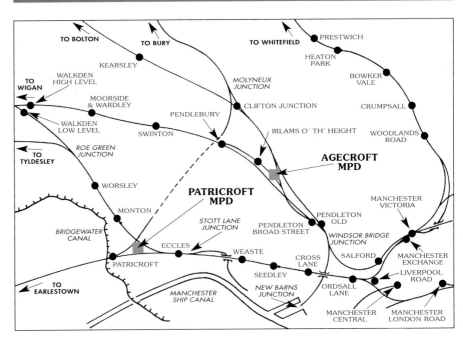

The tower of Manchester Cathedral rises high above Leyland TD5 No **3953** standing at the top of Exchange Station Approach - the terminus of Service 95. This Manchester Corporation vehicle, introduced in 1940, had Metro-Cammell/Crossley bodywork and this particular example was one of the last of the batch of 83 to go - being withdrawn in 1962 - by which time it had moved on to Queens Road Garage. Service 95 was the responsibility of Parrs Wood Garage at the time of the photograph and No 3953, which was allocated there, is awaiting departure with an outward bound journey to East Didsbury. Shortly afterwards, operation was taken over by nearby Birchfields Road Garage whose Crossley vehicles replaced those of Parrs Wood, who had utilised buses of both Crossley and Leyland origin.

1951 ● ROY MARSHALL

The austere station entrance stands beyond the parked cars and replaced the war damaged original LNWR structure featured in the earlier photographs (page 3). A part of the ex-L&YR headquarters, with its ballustraded arch at neighbouring Victoria Station is visible above the canopy. The Birchfields Road conductor, complete with 'Ultimate' ticket issuing machine, is standing on the platform of Daimler CVG5 No **4490** and is obviously aware of the cameraman's presence! This bus was unique in having Metro-Cammell lightweight 'Orion' bodywork and lightweight chassis. It represented Manchester Corporation at the Earls Court Commercial Vehicle Motor Show before introduction into traffic in October 1955 The following month, Service 95 was extended to run jointly with Salford City Transport between East Didsbury and Whitefield (via Broughton Bridge). A parallel service, No 96, was also introduced and ran via Strangeways. Both these new cross-city routes were re-directed to pass through Victoria Bus Station, making this photograph something of a rarity.

OCTOBER 1955 ● A. HAYNES COLLECTION

Manchester Exchange Station first opened on 30th June 1884 as a result of the ever increasing congestion at neighbouring Victoria. Although the platform accommodation had doubled there, it remained insufficient to deal with the traffic of both LNWR and L&Y. The L&Y insisted on full ownership and whilst the LNWR retained certain rights, the North Western Board built the adjacent Exchange, named after the 'Cotton Exchange', situated in nearby Hanging Ditch and a trading centre of worldwide renown within the industry. It was their second major station in the city, following London Road which handled traffic to the south. Exchange was situated on the west side across the city boundary formed by the River Irwell and, as a consequence, was in Salford. In many respects it was an annexe of Victoria and the combined area covered by both stations fell just short of being Britain's biggest. That honour belonged to London's Waterloo by half an acre! Mr. Francis Stephenson, Designer-in-Chief of the LNWR, developed the building whose white stone Italianate styled frontage occupied a commanding position facing Manchester Cathedral. The broad bridge from Victoria Street over the river offered main access and was known as Cathedral Approach. An alternative entrance parallel to the train shed was by way of Chapel Street which was known as the Salford Approach. In addition, a steep flight of steps led from Greengate to the top of the approach roads. Direct access on to Platforms 4 and 5 for parcels traffic could be gained from a carriageway at the junctions of Chapel Street and Victoria Street under which the River Irk joined the Irwell. Station facilities included Booking Offices in a block near the main entrance, facing which were various Departmental Offices and Waiting Rooms. The licensed Refreshment Rooms were on the side facing Victoria Street.   **1910 ● JOHN RYAN COLLECTION**

In 1910 there were 121 departures to various destinations which included Liverpool, Chester, North Wales, Holyhead (for Ireland) and Yorkshire. Suburban services operated to Bolton and Wigan. By 1914 the booking office had moved on to the main concourse behind the stop blocks of the bay platforms Nos 1 and 2. The through platforms, Nos 3, 4 and 5 are to the right. Signage on the LNWR was good and the station was blessed with several large clocks. A staff of nearly 300 comprised platform and ticket staff, telegraph office, parcels and carriage department, kitchen and refreshment, signalmen (2 boxes) and guards. By 1965 daily departures had reduced to 85 and staffing levels were significantly reduced.

1914 ● MANCHESTER CENTRAL LIBRARY

The station suffered badly from the ravages of war. The main building and train shed took a direct hit during the blitz of December 1940 and never really recovered. This view looking up Cathedral Approach reveals a series of bricked up archways which once formed a grand entrance on to the concourse. The wooden hut acting as a makeshift ticket office and now fronting the building was supposedly a temporary measure but was still in situ nearly twenty five years later! The station car park on the approach road is full, accommodating a mere fifteen cars, the pick of which must be the model sports car. Meanwhile Strangeways tower manages to creep into yet another photograph.

9th OCTOBER 1964 ● GRAHAM WHITEHEAD

LNWR DAYS

LNWR 'Prince of Wales' 4-6-0 No 321 *Henry W. Longfellow* was the 21st member of a large class of 246 locos and was introduced in November 1913 as one of the initial Crewe batch of 135 members. The onset of the 1914-18 War dictated that the remainder were built by outside contractors as Crewe became engaged in other areas appertaining to the war effort. As a resident of Llandudno Junction shed, No 321 was a regular performer on the Manchester 'Club' train and was kept in immaculate condition there. Having arrived on time earlier in the day with the ex-Llandudno, the engine then retired to Patricroft Shed where a thorough examination, in addition to normal servicing took place. It is about to reverse on to the stock ready for a prompt 4.30pm departure for home. The engine and train crew were apparently threatened with fines for late arrival in connection with this train but whether any were actually implemented remains unrecorded. No 321 was withdrawn in January 1935. **c.1920 ● PAUL SHACKCLOTH COLLECTION**

A rare view showing semaphore signals in the vicinity of Exchange Station. All were replaced two years after this photograph was taken by four-aspect colour light signals and power operated points in what was the first major installation of its kind outside the London area. Whale 'Precursor' 4-4-0 No **234** *Pearl* stands just beyond the train shed awaiting her next duty. It is still running as originally built in March 1906 and the newly formed LMS company took over three years after the Grouping before re-numbering the first unrebuilt examples of the class. No 234 became LMS No 5237 in December 1927 and was withdrawn in February 1932.

7th JUNE 1926 ● H.C. CASSERLEY

In LNWR days, a 45ft turntable was situated immediately west of Platform 1, offering smaller engines a convenient turn round facility. The table certainly couldn't accommodate this 'Cauliflower' Goods 0-6-0 tender engine which had come to grief. The probable explanation is that No **1160** was bringing empty stock into the station only to find the points wrongly set. Although the tender has reared up over the stop blocks, the engine appears not to have derailed and damage may be minimal - the signalman responsible would certainly have been hoping so. The two short spurs in the foreground were holding sidings.

10th JUNE 1912 ● JOHN RYAN COLLECTION

LNWR 5' 6" 2-4-2T No 338 emerges from the gloom and into the daylight with a stopping train. The engine was a member of a class of 160 and was built in 1892, becoming LMS No 6640 at the Grouping. It was withdrawn from service in 1931. Of particular interest is the six wheeled stock, the leading coach being a 32ft lavatory brake composite. Torpedo ventilators are in evidence on the roof which were an addition in the late 1890's and the lower footboard has been removed save for a small section in the middle. The well of the small turntable situated here is just visible in front of the engine.   **c.1905 ● PAUL SHACKCLOTH COLLECTION**

Is this a case of the L&Y encroaching on to LNW territory? The photograph is undated but it may well be 1922, the year before the Grouping when these two companies amalgamated. The Barton Wright large wheeled 0-6-2 side tank No **273** built by Kitson, marshalling a through Caledonian coach towards Exchange's platforms might be one of the Victoria Station Pilot engines on transfer duty. Alternatively, it could be acting as the Exchange Pilot. Also of interest is one of the original LNW signalboxes in the area, supported on a gantry straddling the approach roads.   **c.1922 ● A.G. ELLIS**

LMS DAYS

Ex-LNWR Webb-built 'Waterloo' Class 2-4-0 No 5097 *Adelaide* impatiently blows off steam before drawing its clerestory stock out of the station. During the LMS period, Crewe Works fitted smokebox plates to certain pre-grouping locos only, but prior to this it had never been LNWR practice to do so. They were favoured by the Midland so that their engines could be easily identified within a roundhouse, a style of engine shed largely adopted by that Company. Similarly, the Great Western Railway locos carried front numbers on their bufferbeams. No 5097 was a long standing resident of Patricroft and carries a circular LMS emblem on its cab sides. These popular engines were also known as 'Whitworths' or 'Small Jumbos'.

6th JUNE 1927 ● L.W. PERKINS

The elegance of ex-LNWR 'George the Fifth' 4-4-0 Class No 25350 is seen to great effect here. The loco is in immaculate condition and was destined to become the last survivor of a class originally numbering 90 members. They were built at Crewe from 1910 and were superheated versions of the earlier 'Precursor' class. No 25350 was introduced into service as number 868 in June 1911 and received the name *India*. In 1927 the LMS renumbered it 5350 and it was further renumbered 25350 in July 1936. Two months later the nameplates were removed in favour of the newly intro-duced Stanier Jubilee No 5574. With impending Nationalisation, the loco was allocated BR number 58011 in March 1948, but in the event did not carry it as the loco was withdrawn two months later, rendering the class extinct.

1937 ● W. POTTER

The Whale 4-6-0's were divided into two groups. The 19" Goods were widely distributed over the former LNWR system whilst the passenger engines were the 'Experiment' Class - a direct development of the 'Precursor' design. Patricroft shed had six 19" Goods and four 'Experiments' to call on in pre-grouping days, but by 1938 had only three of the former. One of these, No **8815** is standing in Platform 4 on Station Pilot duty. The goods engines were destined to become the last representatives of the 680 LNWR locos with 4-6-0 wheel arrangement. No 8824 of Springs Branch, Wigan survived until February 1950, at which time the class were rendered extinct. Once again, BR numbers were allocated to the last four members but were never carried.

MAY 1938 ● W. POTTER

Ex-LNWR 'Prince of Wales' Class 4-6-0 No
5727 stands at the throat of Exchange Station before
reversing on to its train. In 1930 Patricroft still had 20
members of the class to call on but the arrival of
Stanier locomotives later in the decade, particularly the
Class Fives, quickly eclipsed these passenger tender
engines. The distinctive outline of Threlfall's Cook
Street Brewery is prominent beyond the recently
opened Deal Street Signalbox. Smoke emissions from
both the Brewery and locomotive chimneys help create
the industrial atmosphere that was so typical of much
of the city of Salford. **1930** ● **J.M. BENTLEY COLLECTION**

LMSR Class 4F 0-6-0 No 4359 blows off steam
awaiting departure with a westbound stopping train
which includes a box van of North Eastern origin behind
the tender. These Fowler locomotives were frequently
used on passenger train working, despite being classified
4F, and were first introduced in 1924. They had left-
hand drive, unlike their earlier Midland counterparts.

29TH AUGUST 1927 ● **L.W. PERKINS**

A fine atmospheric photograph of a
Jubilee still in ex-works condition. No **5650**
entered service on 14th January 1935 at
Crewe but went to Shrewsbury and Camden
before arriving at Patricroft on 4th January
1936. It stayed until 22nd May 1937 during
which time it received the name *Blake* on
18th February earlier that year. No 5650 is
about to get a Holyhead parcels train away
from Platform 4 - a duty which had been in
the hands of a 4-6-0 'Prince of Wales' or
4-4-0 'George the Fifth' engine for many
years.

4TH APRIL 1936 ● **R.S. CARPENTER**

A Llandudno Junction LMS Compound 4-4-0, No 1093 showing Express Passenger headlamps, departs from Platform 4 with a train whose first two carriages are of non-corridor stock!
20th MARCH 1948 ● A. HAYNES

The prototype of a class that were later referred to as 'Baby Scots'. This loco was a nominal rebuild of ex-LNWR Claughton 4-6-0 No 5971 *Croxteth* which was withdrawn after a collision on 6th March 1930. It continued to carry that number after completion at Derby in November 1930, but the original *Croxteth* name was not restored until October 1933. As part of the 1934 renumbering scheme, it became No **5500** in 1934 and continued to carry the nameplates. On 25th February 1937 it was renamed *Patriot* with new plates after the withdrawal of Claughton 4-6-0 No 5964 (ex-LNWR No 1914) in March 1934. Both sets of PATRIOT nameplates carried the supplementary wording 'In memory of the fallen LNWR employees 1914-1919'. No 5500 (1B Camden) stands in Platform 3 coupled to an ex-LNWR dining car. **MAY 1936** ● **W. POTTER**

Making a dramatic entrance into the station is Farnley Junction Jubilee 4-6-0 No **5704** *Leviathan* with a stopping train from Leeds. In 1946, this ex-LNWR shed had four examples to call on: Nos 5702/4/5/8, but in the early BR period, three of these were transferred away. No 45702 *Colossus* went to Newton Heath in December 1950 and No 45705 *Seahorse* to Blackpool in June 1956, after which it became a regular visitor on the residential services. *Leviathan*, however, went to Carlisle Kingmoor in October 1952 and locally, little was seen of it until June 1959 when the Jubilee transferred to Crewe North. At the same time (October 1952), the shed received Nos 45581 *Bihar and Orissa*, 45646 *Napier* and 45695 *Minotaur*. The other one, No 45708 *Resolution* stayed at Farnley Junction throughout.

18th OCTOBER 1946 ● **H.C. CASSERLEY**

Hall Class 4-6-0 No 4959 *Purley Hall* departs from Manchester Exchange Station with an express for Chester. Over 100 different members of the class have been recorded in the area since their introduction in 1928.   1938 ● R.S. CARPENTER COLLECTION

GREAT WESTERN ENGINES IN THE MANCHESTER AREA

The Great Western Railway reached Manchester in 1860, having previously made an unsuccessful attempt to establish a foothold in the city via the southern approaches from Walton Junction, Lymm and Timperley Junction. Chester had been reached five years earlier by way of their own tracks to Saltney Junction and then by exercising running powers over the LNWR system. A similar arrangement existed east of Chester via Walton Junction and Earlestown through to Manchester. During the LMS period, classes of locomotive permitted to work over the section were: 'Saints', 'Halls', 'Dukes', 'Bulldogs', 'Moguls' and all manner of 0-6-0's. Officially prohibited were members of the 'Grange', 'Manor' and 'Castle' class, but the former were observed on many occasions. Although Kings were banned north of Shrewsbury, Castles were regular visitors to Chester. The only known occasion of a visit of a member to Manchester occurred during the afternoon of June 23rd 1936 when No 5054 *Tretower Castle*, coupled to Grange No 6812 *Chesford Grange* and a GWR Engineer's saloon arrived at Exchange Station at 3.16pm for clearance tests, departing for the west one hour later. In the 1920's, motive power consisted of 'Badmintons', 'Cities', 'Flowers', 'Atbaras', 'Bulldogs' and No 4171 *Armstrong*, which appears to have been the most common visitor - but by the 1930's it was mainly 'Halls', 'Saints' and 'Moguls'. However, unprecedented visitors on Patricroft shed included a 'Star' Class in 1932, No 4027 *Norwegian Monarch* and a 28XX, No 2828 during 1933. Interesting double-headed trains which consisted of various ex-LNWR and GWR types were also observed. One such combination was 'Precedent' No 5001 *Snowdon* piloting 'Bulldog' No 3338 *Swift* into Exchange from North Wales on August Bank Holiday Monday, 1931. On another occasion in 1935, engines of the same number were in tandem - 'Precursor' No 5316 *Viscount* piloting 'Mogul' No 5316. A 'King' did appear in 1930 in conjunction with the Liverpool & Manchester Centenary celebrations when No 6029 *King Stephen* was involved (see page 70) and Castle Class Nos 4082 *Windsor Castle* and 5006 *Tregenna Castle* were both on Longsight Shed when they were shown at the 'Railway Carnival' at Belle Vue Gardens in 1925 and 1932 respectively. The outbreak of war curtailed much GWR activity and many workings became the responsibility of Chester LMS shed.

Saint Class 4-6-0 No 2950 *Taplow Court* enters Manchester Exchange Station with a stopping train. 37 different 'Saints' were observed during the LMS period, but as the class were introduced in 1902, it seems likely that many more visited the area.   1931 ● J.M. BENTLEY COLLECTION

The post-war period brought various sightings of GWR engines in and around the Manchester area. During the *1948 Locomotive Exchanges*, Hall Class No 6990 *Witherslack Hall* worked on the ex-Great Central main line between Manchester London Road and London Marylebone. A 'ROD' 2-8-0 No 3038 from Pontypool Road was observed on Trafford Park Shed on 18th November 1955, having worked in via Helsby, Northwich and Altrincham. A report in *Trains Illustrated* mentions Hall Class No 5916 *Trinity Hall* passing through Heaton Chapel towards London Road on the evening of 20th December 1955. An outstanding visitor on 27th October 1959 was 0-6-2T No 5611 from Croes Newydd, which worked the 6.25am Chester Northgate to Altrincham train. The loco off this train normally returned with the 8.20am Altrincham to Northwich then empty stock to Chester. On this occasion, No 5611 came off at Altrincham and proceeded light engine to Heaton Mersey shed, where it spent a few days. There is no record of how or when the engine returned home.

'Atbara' Class 4-4-0 No 4139 *Auckland* is shrouded in steam as it prepares to leave the station with an express working. Regular departures behind GWR locos throughout the 1920's and 1930's were as follows:

11.00am to Chester.
ex-7.55am Chester to Exchange (arr 9.08am)

5.08pm(SX) local to Newton-Le-Willows.
ex-2.35pm Chester to Exchange (arr 3.45pm)

10.20pm to Holyhead.
The engine for this train arrived with the 5.30pm freight from Saltney to Patricroft and Ordsall Lane. In addition, the engine off the 5.13pm Chester to Exchange passenger returned on the 7.45pm Liverpool Road to Bristol freight. The northbound freight arrived in the early hours at 6.00am whilst other GWR locos (usually Moguls) could be seen in the area at various times on local goods services.

1925 ● ALLAN SOMMERFIELD COLLECTION

GWR locos were regularly observed on the 1.45pm train to Holyhead, although the inward working could not be established. Dukedog Class 4-4-0 No **3212 Earl of Eldon** awaits departure from Platform 2 with the train. The engines working into Exchange on regular passenger trains made use of the turntable and watering facilities at Ordsall Lane, by No 2 signalbox. One of the signalman's duties was to record the GWR loco numbers as the LMSR levied a charge of 1/0d for the privilege of topping up the tank. During the layover period they stood on one of the spare roads but were occasionally used on empty stock workings from Ordsall Lane.

MAY 1937 ● W. POTTER

GWR Mogul No 6332 awaits departure with a train bound for Chester. No fewer than 65 examples of this class have been recorded in and around the area, including the last two engines observed on Patricroft shed during the war years. Nos 6329 and 6337 were there on 12th September 1942, one of which would have been used on the evening Bristol freight. Engines always seemed to be stabled in the 'old' shed and whilst they replenished their tenders with water, they very rarely took coal - which would, no doubt, have been charged for by the LMSR at a premium rate.

MAY 1937 ● W. POTTER

The 4.30pm 'Club Train' to Llandudno arrived on the coast at 6.45pm, having called at Warrington, Chester, Prestatyn, Rhyl, Abergele, Colwyn Bay and Llandudno Junction. Those business-men who were unfortunate enough to miss this train could catch the 5.07pm stopping train to Chester which connected with the 5.10pm ex-Liverpool Lime Street to Holyhead, arriving at Llandudno Junction at 7.39pm. Stanier Class Five 4-6-0 No **44780** is at the head of the next available through train, the 5.35pm to Llandudno which was all stations to Chester (except Eccles), eventually arriving on the North Wales coast three hours later. The driver keeps still for the necessary time exposure calculated by local photographer John Clarke. The result oozes the atmosphere of a chill winter's evening with Christmas rapidly approaching. The unmistakeable silhouette of the parachute water tank situated towards the end of Platform 2 is evident, whilst the colour light signal and monitor within the station roof shine brightly, as do the clock faces of Trinity Church on Chapel Street.

21st JANUARY 1964 ● **JOHN CLARKE**

The Springs Branch engine crew have just received details from the guard after which all three are prepared to pose for the camera before departure with a stopping train to Wigan North Western.

21st JANUARY 1964 ● **JOHN CLARKE**

The 9.50am stopping train from Warrington Bank Quay arrives at its destination on time at 10.45am behind Mold Junction Class Five 4-6-0 No **45130**. Even though smoke emissions are high, this lightweight train, which had travelled via Tyldesley, would have posed few problems for the Stanier engine but a different challenge lay ahead. In May 1953, along with seven others in the class, the loco was temporarily transferred to Nine Elms on the Southern Region before returning to Mold Junction two months later. *(see No 45223 on page 16)*
9th FEBRUARY 1952 ● **TOM LEWIS**

Both Driver and Fireman are making last minute checks around their engine before departing from Platform 3. The train is the 1.40pm to Bangor, where Class Five 4-6-0 No **44821** is allocated. Lingering smoke within the trainshed had been a problem for years, especially after 1929 when Exchange No 3 and Victoria No 11 platforms were joined to form the longest continuous platform in Europe. Engines hauling the heavy trains departing from Platform 11 Middle often made an understandably volatile start. They were immediately faced with a scissors crossover to gain access to the through road between Platforms 3 + 4, engulfing passengers with smoke in the process. Closer inspection of some of the older photographs taken from a similar vantage point reveal missing panes which had broken within the glazed wall of the canopy roof. A similar problem existed at neighbouring Victoria on Platform 12 where the 'Wallside Pilots' were stabled. By the Spring of 1964, some panes had been replaced whilst others had been systematically removed over the middle roads to improve ventilation.

27th JULY 1964 ● **JOHN CLARKE**

The extension of Platform 1 completed in early LMS days provided the perfect vantage point to photograph trains leaving for the west. On this occasion, Patricroft Jubilee No **45563** *Australia* is at a standstill. Trains arriving in Platform 3 that were of nine carriages or more had to overshoot the platform to clear the scissors crossover connecting Platform 11 Middle. The corridor stock in the background is stabled within the two road Irwell Bridge Carriage Sidings. This could be infuriating for trainspotters as the Up and Down Fast lines serving Victoria were hidden and they were sometimes unable to record traffic passing by. This often resulted in a quick hike down Platform 11 before the loco pulled away with empty stock towards Red Bank. **1955 ● C.C. BERGSTRAND**

Bursting out of the train shed into bright sunlight is Stanier Cless Five No **45435** of Newton Heath Shed which still retains LMS lettering on its tender and would have been one of the last to do so on BR by this time. The train is the 10.30am express to Southport calling at Wigan Wallgate only. Irwell Bridge Signalbox and a parachute water tank can be seen through the gap in the wall which was another favourite location for those side-on shots. Whilst two boys admire the spectacle, the third seems more interested in photographer Tom Lewis's activities. **9th FEBRUARY 1952 ● TOM LEWIS**

The 3.50pm Manchester Exchange to Earlestown local passenger is in the hands of Standard Class 4MT 2-6-0 No **76077** from Sutton Oak shed. These engines were a development of the Ivatt '43000' Class and 115 locomotives were built at Horwich and Doncaster Works from December 1952. Nos 76075-9 were delivered new to the St Helens shed in December 1956 and the engine was destined to spend its entire life in Central Lancashire, transferring to nearby Springs Branch, Wigan, when Sutton Oak closed on 19th June 1967. No 76077 has been preserved on the Gloucestershire - Warwickshire 'heritage' railway. **3rd AUGUST 1957 ● B.K.B. GREEN**

The numerous Stanier Class Fives could be seen over many parts of the BR system, especially during the summer months when members visited such places as Scarborough, Great Yarmouth and South Coast resorts with excursion traffic. Their great versatility prompted the loan of seven of the class to the Southern Region whilst the Merchant Navy Pacifics were temporarily withdrawn from service after the discovery of a serious defect to the axles. No **45223** was based at Bournemouth Shed in May 1953 and retained its 26A shedplate whilst working the crack Waterloo expresses - complete with SR headcode discs. After its return, the loco was involved in a derailment at Droylsden Station on 22nd November 1956 whilst working the 12.55pm passenger train from Manchester Exchange to Leeds City. The loco and six coaches suffered little damage, coming to rest in the station platform. There were no casualties. No 45223 is on more mundane work here - taking empty stock out of Platform 3 for Ordsall Lane. The Station Announcer's office is situated on Platform 1 behind the engine. **MAY 1955 ● GRAHAM WHITEHEAD**

The Manchester Exchange to Bolton Great Moor Street local service had always been primarily the responsibility of Plodder Lane shed. During the LNWR and early LMS periods, a number of Webb 4' 6" 2-4-2T's were utilised, but after their withdrawal, the shed had nothing larger than the 0-6-2 'Coal Tanks' to call on - which Patricroft men always referred to as the 'Plodder Claughtons'. The advent of Nationalisation was very much to the sheds advantage as firstly, Ivatt Class 2MT 2-6-2T's Nos 41210-17 arrived in 1948, replacing the ageing 'Coal Tanks' within the year, and five years later, Plodder Lane had the distinction of receiving the first five members of the Standard version, Nos 84000-4, ex-Crewe Works in July 1953. No **84004,** barely two months old, is departing for Bolton - but the service was short lived as both Great Moor Street Station and Plodder Lane closed on 10th October 1954.

26th SEPTEMBER 1953 ● P. HUTCHINSON

Springs Branch engines had always been a regular sight in the station, working in with local trains. One of their Stanier Class Five 4-6-0's, No **45296** waits in the centre road before returning home. Exchange's No 3 Platform gives way to 11 Middle in bright sunlight at a point under the footbridge. The crossover allowed for independent operation and a similar arrangement existed further down the platform between Victoria's Platform 11 and 11 Middle.

1966 ● D. PASS

This view looking west two years later records Stanier Class Five 4-6-0 No **45156** *Ayrshire Yeomanry* taking on water whilst engaged on station pilot duties. By 1968 there were periods of little activity and an air of gloom hung over the place which was threatened with closure. When the inevitable happened on 5th May 1969, neighbouring Victoria easily accommodated the remaining services and benefited from a facelift at the same time.

20th JUNE 1968 ● PAUL SHACKCLOTH

An all too familiar sight in BR days was that of an unkempt Austerity 2-8-0 on freight duty. This unidentified example is caught trundling through the station heading towards Ordsall Lane with a mix of wagons. In all likelihood, this engine is from Yorkshire, based at either Wakefield, Mirfield or Normanton as Newton Heath, Agecroft and Bolton had cleared their stocks a month earlier in favour of Stanier 8F 2-8-0's.

17th NOVEMBER 1964 ●
GRAHAM WHITEHEAD

The engine that came home. Standard Class Five 4-6-0 No **73096** went new to Patricroft shed in November 1955 before moving on to Shrewsbury in 1958 and spent most of its days working over lines of the former Great Western Railway. After several transfers between sheds, No 73096 returned to Patricroft in July 1965 from where it was withdrawn in November 1967. The loco is now preserved on the *Mid-Hants Railway.* The iron railings in view behind the platform seats protect the inclined plane offering road access on to Platforms 4 and 5 from the corner of Chapel Street and Victoria Street, directly over the River Irwell.

19th JUNE 1965 ● G. HARROP

Stanier Class Five 4-6-0 No 45248 (5B) threads through the middle road with a transfer freight from Ashton Moss to Ordsall Lane. The 'hole in the wall' of the Exchange Station train shed was a legacy of the early LNWR days when a scissor crossing was in-situ from the avoiding line, offering access and departure points midway along Platform 5. **16th APRIL 1964** ● **GRAHAM WHITEHEAD**

More transfer work involves Standard Class Five No **73069**. The loco has run round its train and was about to depart for Ordsall Lane having previously arrived from Brindle Heath. When Exchange Station opened in 1884, a wooden footbridge connected Platforms 2/3 with 4/5 and would have passed over somewhere near the Brake Van buffering up to the loco. This was soon replaced by the wider, wrought iron structure seen in the distance which was more conveniently situated. After Exchange's closure in 1969 and subsequent demolition, this footbridge stood in splendid isolation but open to the elements.

1967 ● **ERIC HUMPHREY**

THE LLANDUDNO CLUB TRAIN

The empty stock off the morning 'Club' train is bound for Ordsall Lane Carriage Sidings, but it was unusual to find a Llandudno Junction engine performing this duty. A possible explanation might be that Stanier Caprotti Class Five No **44738** was 'stopped' on Patricroft shed with a minor mechanical problem after arriving with the previous day's train. If so, Patricroft would have provided a locomotive at short notice which would have returned with this train. The empty stock working might have been a way of a testing for No 44738 before its return on the 4.30pm later in the day. BR were conscious that everything had to be 'just right' with regards to the 'Club' train.　　**17th MARCH 1954** ● **B.K.B. GREEN**

The most prestigious departure from Exchange Station was the 4.30pm Businessman's Train to Llandudno. This long established service dated back to LNWR days and in the later BR period, Llandudno Junction Shed always provided an immaculate Stanier locomotive. The stock was impressive too and included special saloon cars. Caprotti Class Fives Nos 44738 - 40 together with No 45282/85 and 45311 in later years were the most regular performers. Bert Pilkington lived at Llandudno Junction, near the station, and was a daily commuter to Manchester. He worked at various agencies in the advertising industry as a retouching artist. These are a few of his recollections:

The train always used to leave dead on time at 4.30pm and the coaches were spotlessly clean. The people that travelled always sat in the same seats and it took some time before you were accepted in the 'club' and had a regular seat of your own. Some compartments had various 'goings on', such as chess and cards. There was a bridge school if I remember. One chap always carried a fancy case loaded with miniature bottles of whisky etc. for anyone who fancied a small libation (at a price of course). Everybody got to know each other and professional advice was frequently exchanged. Many had financial connections and were known as the 'Exchange Wallers'. The driver and fireman were always the same so you got to know them on a friendly basis. At Christmas time, the tender was always loaded up with presents of some kind. When I caught the train in the mornings at Llandudno Junction, it would wait at the level crossing and blow steam. This was the signal for me to run out of the house with a piece of toast and go like hell. 'Good timing again' was the cry of old porter Jack, who then added, 'you'll miss it one day' - but I never did!

Britannia Pacific No 70018 *Flying Dutchman* (5A) departs from Platform 1 with the 5.10pm 'Club' train to Windermere - a regular Crewe North duty at the time. It reached Preston by a little used route, taking the ex-LNWR line through Tyldesley then the Whelley loop to Standish Junction. A train had departed 10 minutes earlier from Liverpool Exchange and both portions combined at Preston for the onward journey.　　**1963** ● **JOHN CLARKE**

Gresley Pacific No 60007 *Sir Nigel Gresley* (61B), making a welcome appearance in the area, departs from Platform 3 with the *A4 Preservation Society Special* to London Paddington via Chester, Shrewsbury and Birmingham Snow Hill. Unfortunately, the weather was particularly poor on the morning that Driver Jack Mason from Newton Heath shed was at the regulator.　　**22nd OCTOBER 1965** ● **JOHN CLARKE**

STATION PILOTS

The Class 2P 4-4-0's were popular locos with the Patricroft men. No **635** is standing alongside the 'traps' - the nickname for the short spur at the east end of Platforms 4 and 5, although it was unusual for the pilot loco to be facing west. Notice the storm sheet, between the cab roof and tender, offering a degree of protection to the crew from the elements. It obviously rained in the summer months in the 1940's as well! Victoria's Platform 12 is visible behind the engine and a wisp of smoke can be seen coming from 635's safety valves as well as from the distant Strangeways tower.

15th JULY 1949 ● **G. SHUTTLEWORTH**

No 40671 was another Class 2P 4-4-0 which arrived at Patricroft from Preston in March 1957. From that month until withdrawal in November 1960, the loco was a virtual ever-present on Exchange Pilot duty. It was replaced the following month by No 40586 from Bank Hall. The engines were sure footed and were most suited to this work as they benefited from having high seats in the cab which allowed the driver to buffer up 'in vision'. No 40671 has returned light engine, tender first, from the summit of Miles Platting bank, having assisted a Yorkshire bound train out of Platform 5. The signalman at Deal Street box has set the points for Horse Dock Siding, a short spur beyond the west end of Platforms 4 and 5 where the pilot was stabled between duties.

8th SEPTEMBER 1960 ● **PETER FITTON**

One of the last engines to perform the Pilot duty was Stanier Class Five 4-6-0 No **45156 *Ayrshire Yeomanry.*** It arrived from Edge Hill in May 1968 to see out time and was involved in a number of railtours during which period it became a candidate for preservation - which unfortunately never materialised. Eleven years previous to this hectic period, No 45156 and sister No 45154 *Lanarkshire Yeomanry* created something of a mild sensation when they unexpectedly arrived at Newton Heath from St Rollox in April 1957. Amongst others, the Glasgow shed had Nos 45153 - 59 on its allocation at the time and why the Scottish named examples came south in the first place remained a mystery. No 45156 achieved more fame by moving on to Bolton shed in December 1962 for six months, becoming the first (and last) named engine to be allocated there.

9th JUNE 1968 ● **PAUL SHACKCLOTH**

Manchester Victoria West and Exchange were re-signalled in 1929 by the Westinghouse Brake and Signal Company. The original manual signalboxes, one of which was an early LNWR example carried on a gantry straddling the lines in and out of Exchange Station, were replaced by power boxes using miniature lever frames as part of the scheme. They were situated at Deal Street, Victoria West Junction and Irwell Bridge Sidings. The signals themselves were a typical four aspect colour light with a theatre type route indicator mounted above. They were of the Westinghouse optical projector type and had no moving parts - the image being projected on to a glass screen. The junction signals were of standard LMS 'cluster' type. The theatre route indicators were occasionally referred to as 'music halls' as their appearance when lit was not dissimilar to those found in theatres to show the act and scene of the plays - they were designed for low speed movements only. Two examples are sited at the end of Platforms 2 and 3 behind the parachute water tank.

1966 ● PAUL JORDAN

As well as re-signalling, there were radical alterations to the track layout, offering greater flexibility. Previously there had been no physical connection between the four lines west of Victoria that passed by Exchange (ex-L&YR) and the four lines out of Exchange Station itself (ex-LNWR). They were referred to as the North and South Lines respectively. Crossovers were installed between the North Slow and South Slow lines in each direction beyond Deal Street Box. The new arrangement allowed trains from Victoria to reach Chester and North Wales (and vice versa) whilst Exchange could similarly despatch or receive trains from the North West and beyond.

Looking back down Platform 1 towards the concourse and entrance. A number of parcels stacked on a platform trolley and a mother whose children are helping with the luggage, act as a reminder of an everyday scene in the days of steam - taken for granted at the time - but fortunately recorded on film by cameramen who looked beyond the locomotive and train.   **6th AUGUST 1966 ● D.E. SHEPHERD**

The Exchange Station Pilot also acted as the Miles Platting banking engine for passenger trains starting out from Exchange Station bound for Yorkshire and beyond. For many years this was the province of Patricroft's 2P 4-4-0's, one of which, No **40631** is standing in front of Deal Street box. All freight requiring assistance up the bank was dealt with by the 'Wallside Pilots' residing at Victoria Station whose locomotives were provided by Newton Heath. The Southern Region box van in the short bay is unusual but the Royal Mail Morris Commercial vans were an everyday sight, gaining access to Platforms 4 and 5 via an inclined tunnel from Victoria Street.   **4th OCTOBER 1958 ● A.C. GILBERT**

IMAGES AT EXCHANGE STATION

English Electric
Type 4 Diesels

D210 was the first member of the second batch (D210-D236) of English Electric Type 4 Diesel Locomotives. They were built at Vulcan Foundry in 1959 and were allocated to the top link sheds on the London Midland Region. The Camden based diesel was named ***Empress of Britain*** at London Euston on 12th May 1960 by Mr. N.R. Crump, President of Canadian Pacific Railways. Five years later No D210 is caught passing through Exchange's centre road with a train of empty stock.

1st AUGUST 1965 ●
GRAHAM WHITEHEAD

D200 made its inaugural run on 18th April 1958 amidst a blaze of publicity. The headboard read *FIRST 2000hp DIESEL. LONDON - NORWICH. PROGRESS BY GREAT EASTERN.* The first 10 in the series (D200-9) worked out of Stratford on the Liverpool Street - Norwich services after a few had been tried at Finsbury Park - the diesel depot servicing Kings Cross and the Great Northern main line. They eventually ousted the Britannia Pacifics, whose feats on the 2 hour service were legendary. The class was 200 strong and as well as a strong presence on the Western Division of the LMR, many were based on the NER and ScR at depots such as Gateshead, York and Haymarket. No **D331** (Crewe North) awaits departure from Platform 4 with an evening parcels train.

1st SEPTEMBER 1963 ● **JOHN CLARKE**

Main line diesels, as they were referred to by the last generation of enthusiasts in the days of steam, were a fairly popular breed. The 'D200's' and the 'Peaks' were among the first to appear in the Manchester area and their numbers soon found a way into the Ian Allan combined volumes alongside those cherished steam engines. The former could be found at the new Piccadilly Station as well as Victoria and Exchange whereas the Peaks were based at Derby and appeared at Manchester Central. No **D215** *Aquitania* awaits departure from Platform 11 Middle with a passenger train whose first coach is a parcels van. The train heating boiler appears to be working overtime with the front of the engine shrouded in steam. Nos D210 - D235 were the only examples to receive names, all of which were taken from recent liners using the Port of Liverpool.

9th OCTOBER 1964 ●
GRAHAM WHITEHEAD

Running light engine in the direction of Agecroft shed is B1 4-6-0 No **61017** *Bushbuck* from Wakefield. Ex-LNER engines were uncommon in the Victoria and Exchange area, although Gorton Class O1/O4 2-8-0's could occasionally be seen - or an ex-works engine on a running in turn, but much of the transfer freight from the Guide Bridge area to Ordsall Lane travelled via London Road (MSJ&A) and Castlefield Junction.
24th MAY 1960 ● K. FAIREY

LIGHT ENGINES - BR DAYS

Ivatt 2MT Class 2-6-2T No 41217 is running round its train after arrival from Bolton (Great Moor Street). The loco was based at Plodder Lane (10D) shed where it arrived from new in November 1948, together with Nos 41210-6, all of which were fitted for push-pull working. No 41217 left for Barrow in September 1951 to share the Foxfield to Coniston branch workings with No 41221. The final regular passenger train from Great Moor Street to Exchange was hauled by Patricroft based Stanier 2-6-4T No 42574 on 27th March 1954.
1949 ● GORDON COLTAS

An everyday sight in the later years of steam were engines at work in a deplorable condition. Apparently this is Stanier 8F 2-8-0 No **48397**, running towards Agecroft shed.
2nd MAY 1966 ● BRIAN CRAMER

Reversing into Exchange Station with a tender full of coal is a stranger, Class 2P 4-4-0 No **40552** belonging to Leeds Holbeck! One assumes that the engine is about to couple on to passenger stock and stray even further off course with a westbound train, possibly to North Wales - after the headlamps had been adjusted. As it was a summer Saturday in August, Patricroft may well have been short of motive power and have borrowed the engine.
3rd AUGUST 1957 ● B.K.B. GREEN

The first of the Polmadie batch of Britannia Pacifics, No 70050 *Firth of Clyde* awaits departure with the morning 9.30am Glasgow. The last five 'Brits' (Nos 70050-54) all went new there in August/September 1954 and were regular visitors on this turn, although Nos 70053/4 left for Leeds Holbeck four years later. The remainder of the class were hardly ever seen at Exchange or Victoria until Newton Heath received Nos 70045/48 in January 1960.   **1958** ● **K. FIELD**

PLATFORM 11 MIDDLE

A 'namer' was always the main attraction to young trainspotters. These two friends admire Jubilee 4-6-0 No **45558** *Manitoba's* name-plate before the loco departs with a parcels train. The nearer of the two glances incredulously towards the camera.   **1963** ● **JOHN CLARKE**

Platform 11 Middle was unique in so far as trains departing from there appeared in both the Manchester Victoria and Exchange timetables. This was a legacy of the pre-grouping days at which time the stations were fiercely independent.

Bank Hall Standard Class 4 4-6-0 No 75032 awaits departure with the 3.30pm to Liverpool Exchange express, calling at Wigan Wallgate only. The loco is carrying a makeshift front numberplate.

15th APRIL 1965 ● **GRAHAM WHITEHEAD**

Prince of Wales Class 4-6-0 No 1542
Marathon stands between Victoria and
Exchange Stations. The shed plate - No 34,
is just visible in the middle of the cab roof
facing the tender, indicating a Patricroft
locomotive. This was a member of a large
class of 246 engines first introduced in 1911.
Only 135 were constructed at Crewe owing
to the advent of the 1914-1918 war and the
remainder were built by outside contractors.
No 1542 entered service in November 1919
- receiving her nameplates nearly 3 years
later. At the time of the photograph, Platform
11 Middle had not yet been developed and
the stations remained physically independent.
Behind the ornate glass walling in the background lay the foot of Hunts Bank approach
to Victoria Station.

1924 ● J.M. BENTLEY COLLECTION

A regular performer throughout the 1950's on the 9.00am Liverpool Lime Street to Newcastle express was Edge Hill's rebuilt
Patriot No **45535 Sir Herbert Walker KCB**. The loco will take the train as far as Leeds City where it will be relieved by an ex-LNER
Pacific or V2 2-6-2 from either Leeds Neville Hill or one of the Tyneside sheds for the continuation to Newcastle Central. The train
reversed at Leeds City and travelled via Harrogate, instead of York.   **1956 ● K. FIELD**

**George the Fifth Class 4-4-0 No
5396 Typhon** brings a Salford bound
coal train through the middle of Victoria
Station. All members of the 90 strong
passenger tender engines carried nameplates and it was unusual to see one of
these engines on freight duty. *Typhon*
spent a further six months in service
before being withdrawn later in the
year. The front end of a Dreadnought
with a dirty chimney and occupying
Platform 12 is just visible.

MARCH 1936 ● W. POTTER

26

Showing a 'Class H' headcode, ex-LNWR 'Super D' 0-8-0 No **49119** has the Victoria East Junction Home and Millgate Distant restricted clearance signals in its favour. The eastbound train is about to attack the notorious Miles Platting bank and will rely on assistance from Stanier 2-6-4T No **42619** which is the leading 'Wallside Pilot'. Behind stands an Ivatt 2-6-0 No **46487** awaiting its turn. The Up and Down through lines carried heavy traffic by day and night but the trailing crossover between the two was very rarely used.

8th SEPTEMBER 1960 ● PETER FITTON

An impressive view of Robinson O4 2-8-0 No 63897 passing through in the other direction with a transfer freight from Dewsnap to Ordsall Lane. The Mexborough loco is in ex-works condition and this will be undoubtedly be a Gorton 'running in' turn. The 'Wallside Pilot' is ex-L&Y 'A' Class 0-6-0 No **52141** which is also a loco of much interest. About 30 members of the class 'flew the nest' away from the Central Division around 1930. No 52141's allocation history after this year reads as follows: 1931 - Gloucester Barnwood, 1934 - Shrewsbury, 1935 - Farnley Junction, 1936 - Shrewsbury, by 1945 - Nuneaton and 1956 - Newton Heath from where the loco was withdrawn in May 1960.

c.1958 ● DAVID YOUNG COLLECTION

IRWELL BRIDGE SIDINGS

The small signalbox situated at the west end of Victoria Station stands over the river on the borders of the cities of Salford and Manchester. It was built to a standard LMS pattern and replaced an earlier L&Y example which was demolished in conjunction with the resignalling scheme in the area during 1929. It obviously controlled the sidings as well as the loco servicing facility here.

c.1970 ● GORDON COLTAS

The old order. The Newton Heath crew take time out to pose on the footplate of L&Y 2-4-2 Radial tank No **869**. The loco was one of the later batch built in 1905 with large bunkers and Belpaire fireboxes. On 9th April 1906, the boiler of this engine exploded whilst passing The Oaks, north of Bolton, working the 9.30pm Stockport to Colne train. The cause was the overheating of a group of 60 stays, 57 of which broke away entirely from the firebox crown. Fortunately, the crew escaped with scalds and slight injuries but this incident didn't detract from Horwich building a further 20 engines which went into service in 1910.

c.1912 ● PAUL SHACKCLOTH COLLECTION

Buffering up to suburban coaching stock in Irwell Bridge Carriage Sidings is LMS Class 4 2-6-4T No **2437,** one of William A. Stanier's taper-boiler 2-cylinder tank engines of 1935. The first eight of the class originally had domeless boilers and low temperature superheaters They were a development of the original Fowler tanks of 1927 and their principal dimensions were identical, apart from the cylinders which were slightly larger. By 1943, 206 examples had been built and were most common in the Manchester and Stoke area, with a number in Glasgow, but they could be found in all regions, except the Western and Southern.

c.1938 ● GORDON COLTAS

One of the Fowler 2-6-2 locos and taken from a similar vantage point, LMS Class 3MT No **15511** is also on empty carriage stock duties. These were indifferent locos, known locally as 'breadvans', whose original purpose was suburban passenger work. Several members (Nos 40021-40) had condensing apparatus for working through the tunnels to Moorgate, London. No 15511 was renumbered 40012 and became a local engine, based at Lees (Oldham) from 1947 - by which time it was motor fitted for working the pull and push branch service from Oldham Clegg Street to Delph. With the impending demise of the 'Delph Donkey', the loco moved east in September 1954, going to Hull Botanic Gardens.

JULY 1931 ● E.R. MORTEN

MANCHESTER VICTORIA DEPARTURES

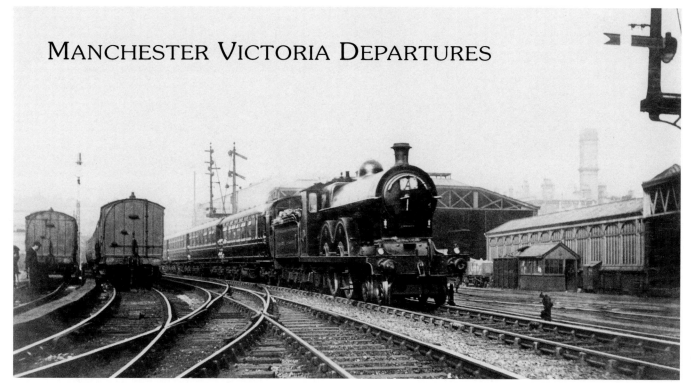

The most spectacular locomotives introduced on the L&Y were undoubtedly the 4-4-2 'Highflyers'. Building commenced in 1899 and by 1902 40 members were in service and 6 years later a quarter belonged to Blackpool shed. They were responsible for the most prestigious train on the system, the 5.10pm 'Club Train' or the 'First Corridor' as it was also referred to. 60 minutes was allowed for the non stop run to Lytham, but according to Mason *(The Lancashire and Yorkshire in the 20th Century)*, the special saloons, known as 'club carriages', also appeared on a later departure at 5.55pm. The photograph shows a 'Highflyer' hauling the special stock but displaying headboard 'A', which was a summer seasonal destination indicator for Blackpool Talbot Road ('B' was for Central). The train is probably the 4.55pm, which was regularly hauled by No 1396. The engine brought in the morning 8.20am express from Talbot Road and called at Bispham and Poulton only. It was then used on a filling-in turn, either a stopping train to Bacup or to Liverpool before returning home with the same stock. This early scene is of much interest showing parts of the original station building and infrastructure.

c.1906 ● JOHN RYAN COLLECTION

Modified Hughes 4 cylinder 4-6-0 No 10432 gets away past Exchange Station with a 'residential' train. The engine entered service in December 1922 carrying standard L&Y numberplates 1661 with LNWR substituted for L&YR. It was one of the last members to be withdrawn in March 1949 from Blackpool shed (28A).

c.1938 ● GORDON COLTAS

The Victoria West End Pilot, which also acted as the standby engine, is seen alongside the Manchester Exchange Station trainshed. Aspinall 4-4-0 No **430** stands resplendent, with all metalwork polished, awaiting its next duty. This engine and sister No 344, which was also kept in a similar condition, had regular drivers for many years right up to the Grouping. During the short period of amalgamation between the L&Y and LNWR (1922), Driver Shaw, who had been in charge of No 344, took the 'Superintendant of the Line', Mr Ashton Davies, into uncharted territory on official visits - north to Carlisle, west to Holyhead and south west down the Hereford line. The formation of the LMS curtailed much of this activity and No 430 resumed ordinary link work.

c.1912 ● PAUL SHACKCLOTH COLLECTION

29

Transfer freights from Patricroft to Brindle Heath
and vice versa to Ordsall Lane and Patricroft were common-
place, with many such movements taking place during the
small hours. Ex-LNWR 'Super D' 0-8-0 No **9052** awaits
the signal, having run round its train, which would consist of
a brake van at either end. **26th MARCH 1948** ● **A. HAYNES**

The West End Pilot in LMS days. Ex-L&Y 'Radial'
2-4-2 Tank **No 10925** rests between spells of activity.
Newton Heath Shed maintained a pre-Grouping tradition of
always turning out a clean loco for this turn. The advent
of World War 2 put an end to this and similar practices
throughout the system.   **c.1936** ● **GORDON COLTAS**

The side elevation of an LMS
standard Compound 4-4-0 displays
much of the elegance surrounding
this class of locomotive. Viewed from
Platform 5 through the convenient
gap in Manchester Exchange's train
shed wall, **No 1104**, a 'Crimson
Rambler', as the locos were fondly
nicknamed, is awaiting the signal
from Deal Street box before making
further progress westwards with a
goods train.   **1935** ● **W. POTTER**

Fowler Class 4 2-6-4 Tank No 2323
passes by Exchange Station light engine on
its way to Agecroft Shed. The engine is
displaying the early LMS, post-1927 10"
numerals with drop shadow lettering. Nos
2312/3/7-22/4 and those members of the
class with side-windows based in Scotland,
were similarly adorned. The Stanier tanks
from No 2425 upwards, other than the
Scottish locos, were given 14" numerals
which had been favoured by the Midland
Railway. No 2323 was at Macclesfield on
31st December 1947 but by 1950 had
moved on to Stoke.

          12th MARCH 1948 ● **H.C. CASSERLEY**

ST MARY'S GATE

Manchester Corporation Tram Service 39 ran from the Exchange terminus (outside the cathedral and adjacent to the station approach) to East Didsbury, travelling via Stockport Road, Slade Lane and Kingsway. Car No **1005** has turned off Deansgate on to St. Mary's Gate and was the second of a large batch (Nos 1004-1053) built in 1927-8 with bodywork by English Electric. The River Irwell formed both the City and operating boundary between neighbouring Manchester and Salford whose remaining trams were about to enter their final month in service. Blackfriars Bridge is just discernable but there was no direct straight-over track connection between the cities at the Blackfriars Junction - a relic of the boundary dispute of 1901-03. The building owned by W. H. Smith & Son, Wholesale Newsagents, standing on the corner of Carr Street and Blackfriars Street, lies just within the Manchester city boundary. **1st MARCH 1947 ● R.B. PARR**

DEANSGATE

Salford Car No 380 had an interesting history. It was built in 1903 as an open-top unvestibuled bogie-car by the English Electric Car Company of Trafford Park for the Trafford Park Estates Light Railway. Numbered 10 in the Trafford Park fleet, it passed to Salford in 1905 and was renumbered 161. It was the decorated and illuminated car chosen for the 1911 Coronation and was the illuminated 'Peace' car to celebrate the end of the Great War in 1919. Six years later it was rebuilt and given an enclosed top cover and platform vestibules. It was further renumbered No 151 in 1931 and again in 1935 when it became No 380. It remained in use until the end of tramway operation - 31st March 1947, latterly appearing in the wartime maroon livery. No 380 is turning off Deansgate on to Liverpool Road whilst working on the Docks Circular - Service 70 - Salford's last tram route. Passing Brown Bros. is one of Manchester Corporation's newly introduced 7ft 6in wide Crossley buses, numbered in the series 2890-2959/61, on Service 48 (Exchange-Altrincham) working out of Princess Road Garage. **1947 ● J.H.S. MORRIS**

MARKET STREET

Having safely negotiated the hustle and bustle of Market Street, Salford Car No **228** is about to pass through Piccadilly on its journey from Kersal to Levenshulme. This was one of a small series (Nos 225-30) supplied by Brush in 1923-4 which were destined to be the last trams bought by Salford and also amongst the last to remain in service (1946-7). No 36 was one of four remaining jointly worked cross-city services with Manchester Corporation, all of which ceased operation in June 1937, traffic congestion on Market Street being a primary factor. The car's condition is commendable and equally noticeable is the policeman's cape on point duty. He is holding up traffic off Mosley Street allowing a multitude of pedestrians to cross between Lewis's (on the left) and the Rylands building.

1932 ● M.J. O'CONNOR

VICTORIA
BUS STATION

In 1899 the authorities in Salford attempted to secure the ground bounded by Victoria Bridge Street, Cathedral Approach and the River Irwell by compulsory purchase in order to create a tram terminus. The London and North Western Railway Company, owners of the land since the opening of Exchange Station in 1884, steadfastly refused, claiming that it would be needed for office extensions, albeit at a lower level. This, of course, never materialised and when the assets of the former LNWR passed into LMS control after the Grouping, a second request was lodged - resulting in purchase in 1935. Victoria Bus Station was then developed, opening in December 1937. Salford's trams were rapidly being replaced by buses and the following year, the number of buses exceeded the number of trams for the first time. The elevated view, taken from the top of Cathedral Approach twelve years later is of interest as it shows the different liveries adopted. Most vehicles are sporting the new green and primrose livery apart from that in the bottom left which is AEC Regent No **157**, still carrying pre-war red and cream. On the far side, the leading bus is showing the wartime red and brown livery.

1949 ● J.A. SOMMERFIELD COLLECTION

Standing in the bus station, awaiting departure are No **254** on Service 73 to Whitefield and No **345** on Service 13 to Agecroft. No 254 is a Crossley DD42/3 with Metro-Cammell bodywork introduced in 1947 whereas No 345 is a Daimler CVD6, also with Metro-Cammell bodywork, brought into service one year later.

12th OCTOBER 1950 ● ABCROSS

Services operating out of Victoria Bus Station in 1968, the last year of steam operation on BR, were as follows:

SERVICE NO	DESTINATION
5	Peel Green (Harrison Street)
7	Sedgley Park (King's Road), via Broughton Bridge - *Part Day*
8	Bolton, via Clifton *Joint Service with Bolton Corporation and LUT*
13/14	Agecroft / Lower Kersal
17	Whitefield (Bus Station), via Broughton Bridge - *Part Day*
20	Higher Broughton (Broom Lane) - *Part Day*
22	Prestwich (Fairfax Road) - *Part Day*
24	Whitefield (Bus Station), via Strangeways - *Part Day*
25	Lancaster Road, via Weaste
27	Monton, via Weaste
28	Monton, via Swinton
30	Lancaster Road, via Pendleton
33	Polefield (Parrenthorn Road)
40	Carr Clough
42	Swinton Park Road - *Part Day*
51	Hillock Estate
73	Whitefield (Bus Station), via Leicester Road
74	Half Way House, via Leicester Road - *Part Day*
82	Half Edge Lane, via Eccles Old Road - *Part Day*
85	Sedgley Park (King's Road), via Strangeways - *Part Day*
95/96	East Didsbury - Whitefield* - *Passes through bus station* *Joint Service. Manchester Corporation and Salford*

NIGHT SERVICES

24	Whitefield (Bus Station)
29	Swinton
68	Peel Green

An interesting period was in 1938-39 when Manchester's Service 77 to Middleton started from Victoria Bus Station bringing pre-war streamline double decks from Queen's Road Garage into the Salford scene.

Several other services left from the adjacent termini at Victoria Bridge Street and Greengate, including in the latter instance some lengthy jointly operated services with Lancashire United Transport, Bolton and Leigh Corporations.

The maroon and cream livery of Bolton Corporation buses offered further variety at Victoria and they worked into the city on the jointly operated Service 8 between here and Bolton via Clifton. The other operators were Lancashire United Transport and Salford City Transport. No **385**, a Leyland Titan PD2/4 built in 1949, awaits return to its home town. Since 1923, Bolton Corporation had purchased both Leyland and Crossley buses in large numbers as well as amassing a sizeable fleet of Daimler vehicles. Forty years later the preferred choice was the popular Leyland Atlantean and their oldest vehicles, the Titans, were in the course of withdrawal by 1965. A member of this 100 strong class, No 408 happily survives - privately preserved in the Bolton area.

1963 ● DAVID YOUNG COLLECTION

In 1951 Salford celebrated 50 years of municipal passenger transport in the city. Daimler CVG6D No **352**, the forerunner of a batch of 87 buses and No 353 were suitably adorned for the occasion. No 430 in the series was similarly adorned but carried raised insignia affixed to the body panels rather than the painted version seen here applied to No 352. Typical examples of the corporate signage utilised by the Transport Department are also evident. SALFORD CITY TRANSPORT BUS STATION and SERVICE 17 are in the green and primrose colours carried by the Salford fleet. Similar bold and distinctive signs, together with those of other local operators, may be viewed at the Manchester Museum of Transport, Boyle Street, Cheetham. In addition, an ever growing number of artefacts, many having been donated by former employees, are on display together with, of course, the preserved vehicles - several of which are in the course of restoration or have been fully restored.

1951 ● DAVID YOUNG COLLECTION

Manchester Corporation Leyland PD2/37 No **3666** is leaving Victoria bus station on Service 95 which was jointly operated with Salford Corporation. It was one of a batch of 40 (Nos 3631-70) buses introduced into service in 1961 with the now familiar Metro Cammell bodywork. Passengers no doubt felt the benefit in the winter months when travelling on these vehicles as they were all fitted with saloon heaters from new. An additional refinement a year later was the fitting of illuminated advertising signs to 14 members of which No 3666 was one. A further two had fluorescent lighting. No doubt the Littlewoods Pools company, amongst others, paid a higher premium for such a facility. All 40 buses transferred into Selnec ownership on its inception on 1st November 1969.

1963 ● R.H.G. SIMPSON

SERVICE No 5
VICTORIA - PEEL GREEN

Three single-deck services were operated by Salford City Transport during the post war years. One such service was No 5 whose outward journey from Victoria was by way of Liverpool Street, Trafford Road in Eccles then under the Bridgewater Canal on Barton Lane (hence the need for single deck buses). The route then followed Peel Green Road to Harrison Street, near Liverpool Road - the terminus. No **69** was an AEC Regal of 1939, with English Electric bodywork and was one of a number of similar vehicles set aside as temporary ambulances in the August of that year - shortly after introduction. The vehicle became a candidate for preservation which unfortunately failed to materialise.

c.1948 ● ROY MARSHALL

The following decade brought replacement vehicles on to the route. No **441** was a Daimler CVG6 of 1950 with bodywork by Burlingham of Blackpool and is standing at the same island shelter within Victoria Bus Station. Standing alongside is one of the S.C.T. service vans which were utilised during the 1950's to carry out emergency repairs to buses on the road, being fully fitted out for the purpose. The van is a Morris LD, one of a fleet of 18 commercial vehicles which all carried the standard livery. Apart from Service 5, single-deck buses operated by S.C.T. were Service 4 - Simister to Prestwich - a part day or intermittent service only, and No 6 which ran from Eccles Bus Station to Radcliffe, although double decks were introduced here in 1951.

c1956 ● J. FOZARD

An example of the final generation of single-deck buses utilised by Salford was No **106**, seen approaching the city terminus. It is one of only nine AEC Reliance vehicles introduced in 1962 which had Weymann bodywork and was to see further service in Colchester after being deemed surplus to requirements. (No 109 of this series is preserved in the St. Helens Museum of Transport). Heading out of town is No **128**, a Daimler CVG6, also introduced in 1962 with Metro-Cammell bodywork. This bus is also on the Peel Green Service, but in this case, Service 64 will pass along Eccles Old Road, Eccles Town Centre and Liverpool Road to New Lane before returning via Winton, Monton and Eccles Old Road as Service 66 to Victoria Bridge. Again, a similar vehicle of this series has happily been preserved within the Manchester Museum of Transport collection. No 112 was the last Salford rear-entrance, open platform bus to remain in service (until 1977, by which time it was SELNEC No 4001).

c.1965 ● DAVID YOUNG COLLECTION

The atmosphere of a winter's evening rush hour is nicely captured here. Drivers, Conductors and Inspectors mingle with the general public, many of whom seem eager not to miss the next bus. The crew of AEC Regent No **147** pose in front of an illuminated vehicle in what must be a staged photograph. Service 66, in common with other principal routes, was strengthened at this time of evening and buses left for Peel Green within minutes of each other. Before the development of Victoria Bus Station in 1937, (behind the shelters and at a lower level). Victoria Bridge Street was a two way thoroughfare and acted as both bus & tram terminus in each direction for many routes. Earlier in the year on 15th February 1949, No 350, a Daimler CVD6 was one of the first buses in the country to be lit by fluorescent tube lights on an experimental basis. Behind the cameraman lies the Grosvenor Hotel on the corner of Deansgate. This was a popular venue for 1st Division football teams playing away at either Maine Road or Old Trafford. Autograph hunters, many armed with *Charlie Buchan's Football Monthlies*, patiently waited for the players to emerge, grabbing their chance before they jumped on the team coach.

NOVEMBER 1949 ● SALFORD LOCAL HISTORY LIBRARY

VICTORIA BRIDGE STREET

Daimler CVG6 No 457 stands resplendent in reversed livery and suitably adorned to mark the Coronation celebrations of Queen Elizabeth II in 1953 *(see overleaf)* is awaiting departure on the circular Service 64 to Peel Green. The outward journey was via Eccles Old Road to Eccles and after reaching New Lane will change to Service 66. The city bound route was via Winton, Monton, Eccles Town Centre and Eccles Old Road.

25th MAY 1953 ● SALFORD LOCAL HISTORY LIBRARY

The last buses to carry the simplified green and primrose livery were a batch of 20 Park Royal-bodied Leyland Atlantean vehicles delivered during the summer of 1969, three months before the inception of SELNEC in November 1969. No **313** is on Service 66 awaiting departure to Peel Green. No 323 of the batch passed into preservation and was first displayed at the Manchester Museum of Transport, in connection with the 'Salford 100' event staged in October 2003. The impressive roof of Exchange Station is prominent together with a part of the ballustraded wall protecting Cathedral Approach. The bus shelter in view ran around the perimeter of Victoria Bus Station with access via steps from Victoria Bridge Street directly behind the Atlantean.

OCTOBER 1969 ● A. RICHARDSON

GREENGATE

By the end of the war, the Salford fleet was in a dire condition. No **147**, a Leyland Titan TD4 of 1936 with Metro-Cammell bodywork, is one of the better examples and is carrying the brown and red livery similarly applied to No **34** parked behind. Other vehicles (both tram and bus) were painted either grey and white, all grey or all brown - such was the lack of conformity. Many were stored unserviceable, awaiting repair and such matters were brought to the attention of the Ministry of War Transport in London who insisted on the adoption of a regular, organised overhaul procedure. With the Greengate and Irwell Rubber Companies premises in the background, both buses are awaiting departure to the Castle Irwell Racecourse in conjunction with a meeting.

1947 ● ROY MARSHALL

The longer distance services tended to congregate in the dank and gloomy Greengate thoroughfare, directly underneath Exchange Station and adjacent to Victoria Bus Station. No **547**, belonging to Lancashire United Transport Limited, is leaving for Westhoughton on Service 38. The route would be via Pendleton, Swinton, Walkden and Little Hulton. The bus is a Guy Arab IV with Northern Counties bodywork, newly delivered in 1955. The shop premises in view are of interest. Flanking S. Aspey - Sweets and Chocolates are Warren-Roberts & Co Ltd., established in 1922 and manufacturers of roller bearings. The counter staff here in the 1960's were renowned for their product knowledge and instant recall of ex-stock items. Just visible by the cab window and bordering on the arches was the unlikely location for The Wool Shop!

1962 ● A. HAYNES COLLECTION

No 456, a Daimler CVG6 of 1951 awaits departure for Weaste Lane on Service 3. This was one of only two buses in the class which were specifically repainted in 'reverse livery' to commemorate the *Salford Civic Week* in 1961 - the other was No 469. Eight years previous, four buses, again of the same class, Nos 437, 457, 458 and 462 were also turned out in reversed livery and suitably adorned to mark the Coronation of 1953. These buses were then used for special tours of Salford later that summer to show the post-war development that had taken place and were subsequently used in normal service until repainted in the normal fleet livery. They were allocated to different routes each week so enabling as many of the Salford public as possible to have the chance to both see and ride on them. Even special commemorative 'Coronation' tickets, illustrating the royal cipher, were issued by the TIM machines carried by the conductors.

1961 ● DAVID YOUNG COLLECTION

Displaying the short lived green and cream livery for this vehicle is Salford No **69**, an AEC Regent with Park Royal bodywork. The bus is at the King Street West terminus in Manchester, ready to leave for Irlams o' th' Height on Service 81. This replaced the 81 tram which had to be abruptly discontinued in May 1944 after storms led to a collapse of the roadway under the tram tracks on Bolton Road, just beyond Pendleton Church. Bus Service 81 was, in turn, withdrawn on 2nd December 1948 and replaced by Service 50 which served the new Duchy Road Estate. Note the familiar lines of the Kendal Milne Department Store in a scene devoid of any other form of transport.

1946 ● ROY MARSHALL

KING STREET WEST

A busier rush hour view looking in the opposite direction towards Bridge Street - at 5.13pm to be precise! A comparison of the rear of these two Leyland PD1's, Nos **293** and **321** is of interest. Two styles of bodywork has resulted in the buses having different apertures to accommodate the blinds. Metro-Cammell have provided the body for No 293 whilst No 321 is an all Leyland product. Both Services 44 and 54 were 'circular' routes, linking King Street West with Eccles Town Centre and Clarendon Crescent, serving Weaste en-route.

19th APRIL 1962 ● **P.J. THOMPSON**

BRIDGE STREET

Only minutes earlier, photographer and bus enthusiast Peter Thompson recorded another rear view around the corner on Bridge Street. A Salford Daimler CVD6 of 1948, No **348**, is about to depart from here on Service 2. This was the city terminus of the long route to Kersal Bar (Moor Lane / Bury New Road) which went via the Docks. The bus ahead about to turn left on to Deansgate then left again on to King Street West is No **293** (see above) on Service 44. Meanwhile, the queue forming outside the Granada Dry Cleaners seems to indicate the popularity of their two hour turn round service.

19th APRIL 1962 ● **P.J. THOMPSON**

MANCHESTER CORPORATION CLEANSING DEPARTMENT

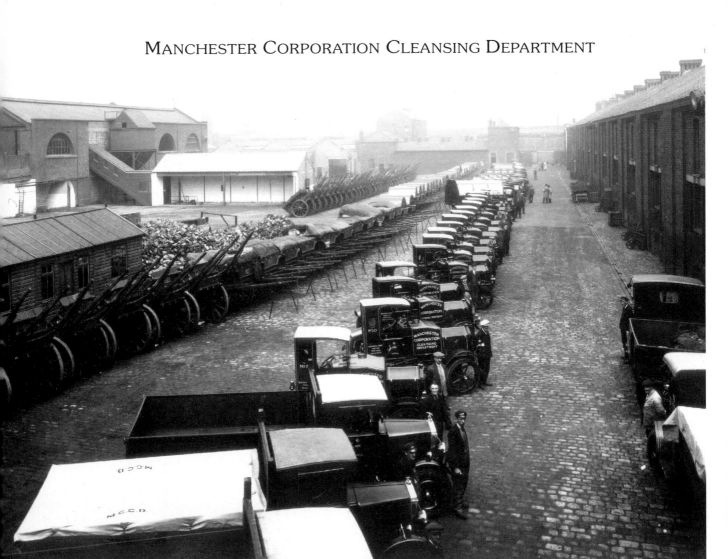

When Salford and Manchester were in dispute over the cross-boundary electric tram services in 1901, Salford cars could not cross Regent Bridge, so the Water Street - Deansgate section had no public service. Manchester made a temporary horse-tram depot in the Water Street yard pending the arrival of electric trams. In later years, Manchester Corporation utilised the premises for their Cleansing Department. A great number of horse-drawn carts are in evidence, neatly aligned behind many of the Manchester fleet of motor vehicles standing ready for official inspection during this transitionary period. Nearby, just beyond the stables to the right lies the pig market and city abattoir. The River Irwell flows immediately behind the warehouse and on the opposite bank is another Corporation yard belonging to Salford, access to which was over Regent Street and down Wilburn Street near Ordsall Lane Station. Ordsall Lane No 1 signalbox is just visible in the background.   **1932 ● A. HAYNES COLLECTION**

CHAPEL STREET

Lancashire United Transport's buses were a common sight in the city but they did not terminate at Victoria Bus Station *(except on Service 8)*. Most long distance and jointly operated routes left from Greengate, directly underneath Exchange Station. No **64**, a Guy Arab IV with Northern Counties bodywork is on Chapel Street having just passed Trinity Church. Service 32, a 'limited stop' journey to Wigan will take 65 minutes, travelling via Worsley, Tyldesley, Atherton and Hindley. Both Salford and Wigan transport undertakings had Road Service Licences for this service as well as LUT who provided all the vehicles. A rather slower service, No 38, which took 78 minutes, connected Greengate with Wigan, following a route through Swinton, Walkden, Westhoughton and Hindley. The railway bridge carrying lines into Exchange Station over Blackfriars Street is just visible.

c.1962 ● DAVID YOUNG COLLECTION

IMAGES AT
SALFORD STATION

A typically deserted Salford Station. It's hard to believe that Platform Tickets *(see below)* were once issued here. The practice of starting trains to East Lancashire from Bay Platform 5 *(on the right)* ceased on 7th October 1957 when services were transferred to neighbouring Victoria. They were the 4.23pm, 5.12pm and 5.25pm to Colne and the 4.50pm to Rose Grove. By 1st May 1961, the station was closed on Sundays and the writing was on the wall. Back in the L&Y period, the 2-4-2 Radial Tanks reigned supreme - none more so than when working the 4.23pm which was considered to be one of the most difficult tasks assigned to locos of this size. Agecroft engines and men worked the train which was made up of ten non-corridor bogies, the gross load often being 260 tons. After traversing the 'Lancashire Alps', first stop was Burnley Barracks before which the rear two coaches were slipped on the descent into Accrington!

1st MARCH 1963 ● GRAHAM WHITEHEAD

Shaded by the canopy, the morning sun catches only the wheels and motion of Stanier Class Five No **45210** easing the 8.30am Liverpool Exchange to Bradford and Leeds express through Platform 3 - the Up Slow line. The scheduled arrival time at Manchester Victoria was 9.20am and departure came 8 minutes later. The train made use of No 13 Platform. On arrival at Low Moor, the Bank Hall Class Five took the front portion on to Bradford Exchange whilst the rear carriages went forward to Leeds Central, often behind a Standard Class 2-6-2 tank. Numbers 84010-15 went 'new' to Low Moor in September 1953 to deal with this work.   **26th SEPTEMBER 1961 ● A.C. GILBERT**

The commercial poster artist has possibly modelled the illustration on Brigitte Bardot in an effort to entice the mainly Lancashire travelling public to sample the delights of Scarborough on the Yorkshire coast. Billboard posters such as these appeared at most BR stations and represented a significant financial income. This example could be found by the exit at the top of the steps on Platforms 4 and 5.

MARCH 1964 ● SALFORD LOCAL HISTORY LIBRARY

The Southport fireman of Fairburn 2-6-4T No 42297 is on the alert for the Salford Starting and Windsor Bridge No 2 Distant signals. His stopping train is the 4.43pm to Southport which consists of three different carriages and a mail van. **1960 ● K. FIELD**

A rather grubby looking 'Crab' 2-6-0 No 42859 passes through the platforms with yet another excursion bound for the Lancashire coast. An enthusiast spending a summer Saturday here (and not many did!) would have been rewarded with an almost constant procession of trains. 'Crabs' would have been plentiful, but this particular loco had an interesting history. It was a long standing resident of Stockport Edgeley shed throughout the 1950's before moving to Willesden in March 1959. It came north again to Birkenhead in 1962 from where it was withdrawn in December 1966. The loco was privately secured from Woodham Bros, Barry and awaits restoration at Binbrook Technology Park, Lincs. It's doubtful if No 42859 handled much passenger work from these depots and will have almost certainly been 'borrowed' on this occasion. The makeshift Reporting Number using a W upside down for M was common practice.

24th AUGUST 1963 ● B.W.L. BROOKSBANK

A second series of twenty ex-L&Y 4-6-0 tender engines were introduced into service during the early LMS period between April 1924 and January 1925. This was as a result of cutting back an original order for thirty Baltic 4-6-4 tanks to ten which had already been built and were proving restrictive. The second member of this batch, No **10456** was temporarily withdrawn in 1926 and rebuilt at Horwich as a four cylinder compound. This was influenced by activities at Derby who, at the time, were contemplating the development of a Compound Pacific. It proved to be Horwich's final involvement in loco design work - the results of which proved economically successful. No 10456 spent much of her time working between Crewe and Carlisle on the West Coast Main Line and used significantly less coal and water than her counterparts. The loco is seen drifting through the platforms, nearing its destination with a Blackpool train.

1932 ● PAUL SHACKCLOTH COLLECTION

The footplatemen on engines departing from Manchester Victoria which travelled on the Down Main were faced with sighting problems whilst passing through the vicinity of Salford station. The island canopy roof restricted the visibility of the normal bracket signal showing Home Starter, Oldfield Road Distant & Splitting Distants. The modification involved the tubular steel dolls being set much closer than the standard six foot spacing and, of course, had shortened arms. In cases such as this, the signal lights were occasionally 'intensified lit' to assist the process. The crew of Blackpool Jubilee 4-6-0 No **45705 *Seahorse*** had no such problems on their approach to Victoria, as the Up lines were controlled by colour light signals at this point. Note the crude, but effective power distribution to the station lamp posts using insulators and suspended wires - a legacy of the Second World War.

28th APRIL 1961 ● H.C. CASSERLEY

Salford Signalbox or Salford Cabin as it was referred to, was situated at the west end of the island platforms (Nos 2 and 3) between the Fast and Slow lines. The 92 lever box closed on 22nd April 1967.

1st MARCH 1963 ● GRAHAM WHITEHEAD

Ex-L&Y Salford Station canopy detail.

1st MARCH 1963 ● GRAHAM WHITEHEAD

A lengthy train of non-corridor stock drifts westbound through Salford Station behind Newton Heath Class Five 4-6-0 No **45336.** The track in the foreground is the headshunt which extends to the platform end, and the Up loop which rejoined the main line here after running from Oldfield Road. It also offered access to the sidings of Manchester Collieries and Manchester Slate Company which were immediately east of Oldfield Road. The Old Bleachers Yard was originally situated behind the wall on the extreme left.

17th OCTOBER 1953 ● TOM LEWIS

The last Saturday of the 1954 Summer Timetable was cold and miserable and, as usual, the 9.30am Manchester Victoria to Glasgow express was double headed as far as Bolton. The train engine was one of the regular performers - Clan Pacific No **72000 *Clan Buchanan*** from Polmadie, Glasgow - and the pilot, Fairburn 2-6-4T No **42151** was from Sowerby Bridge. The pair have just cleared Salford Station after negotiating the severe reverse curves beforehand. They are on the Down Slow line as this train makes use of the connection between Brindle Heath and Agecroft Junctions before regaining the old Bolton route. Another Polmadie Clan, No 72003 *Clan Fraser* was recorded hauling the train the following year in July 1955 when it had the dubious pleasure of a Sowerby Bridge ex-L&Y 'A' Class for company in the shape of No 52410 as part of the same diagram.

4th SEPTEMBER 1954 ● B.K.B. GREEN

SOWERBY BRIDGE MPD
TURN 57

6.30am - 2.35pm   8hrs 5mins

Summer Saturdays Only

ENGINE PREPARED BY TURN 203

SO	LE	6.45am	Shed	Todmorden	7.15am
SO	Pass	7.46	Todmorden	Manchester	8.37
SO	ES	8.47	Manchester	Salford	8.50
SO	Asst	9.30	Manchester	Bolton	9.53
SO	LE	Bolton	Bolton Shed	10.13	
		COAL			
SO	LE	11.30	Bolton Shed	Bolton	
SO	Pass	12.00	Bolton	Sowerby Bridge	2.12
SO			RELIEF 2.15pm for Normanton by TURN 58		

Similar weather conditions were experienced by photographer Peter Fitton who recorded the passage of Stanier Class Five No **44686** on the 4.10pm Manchester Victoria to Southport express at Oldfield Road. Nos 44686 and 44687 were the last two Class Fives to enter service in April/May 1951, both built at Horwich with Caprotti valve gear, Skefco roller bearings and double blastpipes and chimneys. No 44686 was withdrawn from Southport in October 1965. The train is about to pass over the Manchester, Bolton and Bury Canal which had been diverted from its original course in 1890 when the line between Victoria Station and Windsor Bridge was widened. The perimeter fencing in the foreground protects the 'new' canal basin but a complete reconstruction was necessary between Oldfield Road and Windsor Bridge behind a retaining wall. The prominent building through the engine's exhaust is Ordsall Lane Goods Shed which was rail connected by means of a wagon traverser, and apart from a solitary van, Oldfield Road Sidings appear to be empty. The land to the left was once occupied by sidings serving Manchester Collieries Ltd. and Manchester Slate Co Ltd. **31st AUGUST 1965 ● PETER FITTON**

An elevated view of the west end of Salford Station. A Stanier Class Five is nicely framed between signalbox and canopy, with a train for Manchester made up of six blue and grey liveried coaches. Passing under the station is Irwell Street, now a sad shadow of its former self but notice the patch of tarmacadam where the 'Pugs' once crossed.   **22nd APRIL 1966** ● **TONY RENSHAW**

Irwell Street at road level. The spire of St. John's Cathedral and Brown Brothers occupy the background. They were a motor accessory distributor and cycle manufacturer, opening for business on 24th June 1955 but the distinctive building was formerly a jam works. Meanwhile, a Stanier 8F drifts by, tender first, towards Ordsall Lane.   **7th MARCH 1967** ● **DAVE JESSOP**

The former Preston Yard - a part of the Salford goods complex, was bound by the curving viaduct, Stanley Street and Irwell Street. The sheet shed, a large building obliterated during World War 2, once occupied a greater part of this site. The derelict coal stage acts as a reminder of times gone by and on one of the weed infested sidings stand five Freightliner bogies. The yard closed completely in August 1968 after which time it became yet another car park. A Liverpool bound six-car Trans-Pennine set crosses the viaduct. These units were serviced at Botanic Gardens, Hull and when they were first introduced in 1961, a staggering 45% increase in patronage from Leeds alone during the first week of service was recorded. In later years, the six car sets were reduced to five with the loss of the buffet/griddle car facility. The advent of the M62 motorway resulted in a steady decline of passenger numbers and the trains soldiered on until May 1979, by which time they had been further reduced to four cars. They briefly saw service on the Hull and Cleethorpes to Manchester Piccadilly route before withdrawal in 1984. As with the Inter-City Class 123 units, which were withdrawn simultaneously, no examples have been preserved.   **22nd APRIL 1966** ● **TONY RENSHAW**

An aeriel view of the heart of the city of Salford in its zenith. It comes as no surprise that at least six engines can be detected in the area. The ex-L&Y lines show a 10 coach train occupying Platform 1 in Salford Station whilst empty stock, which will form a late afternoon departure to East Lancashire, stands in the bay. A light engine passes Threlfalls Brewery approaching the station on the Down Fast. The former LNWR lines are also busy with two trains passing on the Up and Down Slow over New Bailey Street. A light engine is reversing down to Exchange Station on the Up Fast and another engine, possibly the Station Pilot, can be seen in the vicinity of Deal Street signalbox.   **1930 ● A.W. HOBART**

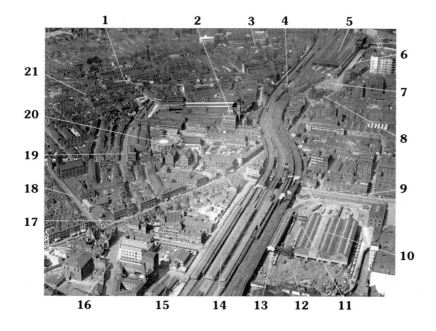

1 - Blackfriars Road
2 - Threlfalls Brewery
3 - Greengate
4 - Deal Street Signalbox
5 - Manchester Exchange Station
6 - Chapel Street Station Approach
7 - Trinity Market Place
8 - Trinity Church
9 - New Bailey Street
10 - New Bailey Street Goods Warehouse
11 - 10 ton Overhead Travelling Crane
12 - New Bailey Goods Yard
13 - Goods Forwarding Shed
14 - Salford Station
15 - Irwell Street
16 - Ordsall Lane
17 - Chapel Street
18 - St. Stephen Street
19 - William Street
20 - Salford Gas Works
21 - Designated 'Play Street' area

IRWELL STREET GOODS

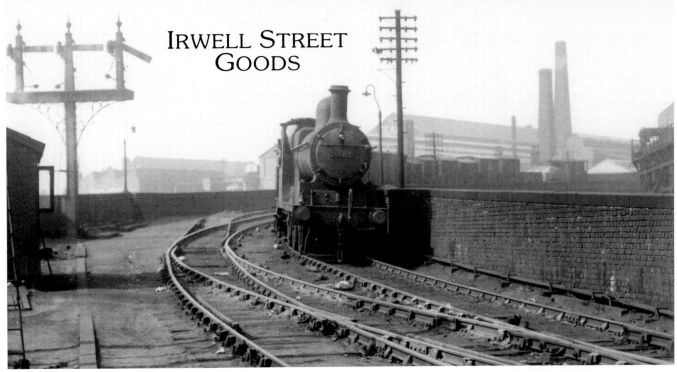

Cautiously descending the 1 in 27 incline from Oldfield Road Junction at no more than 4mph is ex-L&Y 'A' Class 0-6-0 No **12162**. The train of not more than 35 wagons had been previously brought to a stand opposite the shunter's cabin at the top of the incline by Oldfield Road signalbox. The verbal instruction was to then proceed as far as the 'Stop and Wait Instructions' board at the foot of the incline. The Yard Inspector, having satisfied himself that the wagons were secure, may then instruct the driver to detach his engine or to proceed into the bottom yard. Wagons were allowed to be lowered by gravitation under strict instruction - providing sufficient men were in attendance. The Yard Inspector would sound a Klaxon horn, fixed in the goods yard, to give a timely warning to staff working within close proximity. A further regulation stipulated that both lines between the Goods Yard and Oldfield Road box may be used in either direction. The balanced bracket signal is pure L&Y vintage, controlled by the small Salford Goods Yard Signalbox which opened in 1884 although the incline itself predates this by 17 years. The commencement of goods activity at low level is vague but by 1849 at least two towers incorporating hydraulic hoists were operating, capable of handling two wagons simultaneously. The arches of the viaduct were convenient for the deposit of goods together with an assortment of warehouses. **1935 ● REAL PHOTOS**

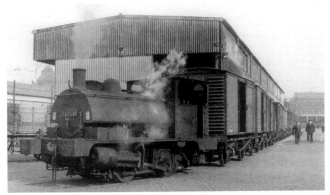

Hard at work in the New Bailey Yard is 0-4-0ST No 51204. A yard shunter with pole in hand approaches the engine whilst chatting to a colleague. All manner of produce passed through the yards other than coal and stone. **24th MARCH 1962 ● G. HARROP**

Standing alongside the coal stage is Jinty 0-6-0 No **47579**. This loco became a regular here after the withdrawal of the last 2F 0-6-0 SaddleTanks (Nos 51408/13), which had supported the 'Pugs' for a number of years. **24th MARCH 1962 ● G. HARROP**

The last active 'Pug' at Irwell Street was No 51232 with No 51237 kept as reserve at Agecroft. It is standing by the Inspector's office prior to crossing the road. The wooden 'dumb' buffers were a feature of these little engines. **9th MAY 1963 ● B. CRAMER**

Another study of a 'Pug' crossing on the level. It's hard to believe that a cab side number exists under the grime but the front numberplate reveals No **51207**, which came to Agecroft from Goole in July 1952. **18th JANUARY 1962 ● R.S. GREENWOOD**

The flagman walks in front of his engine, Pug 0-4-0ST No **51204** which is crossing Irwell Street at no more than 6mph with a maximum of 10 wagons in tow. This was the daytime stipulation between the hours of 5am and 12 midnight with 20 wagons being permitted at other times. Its passage has inconvenienced only two road vehicles going away from the city. A BR 6 ton Scammell Scarab and a Ford Convertible await a clear road ahead, whilst another Scarab is parked alongside the brick wall enclosing New Bailey Yard. The wall is supporting no fewer than 14 billboards, 11 of which are vacant. The nearest three are promoting the various activities at the late and much lamented Belle Vue. The 'Zoo Park' as it was referred to, was of international renown. Popular with youngsters were the sea lions - not forgetting the 'Bobs' and Scenic Railway. On the evening of Saturday, 29th July 1961 there are two sporting attractions. The Kings Hall stages a wrestling programme with Jack Pye versus Gwynne Davies topping the bill. Hans Streiger fights Bob Sweeney in a supporting contest. Meanwhile at the Stadium further down Hyde Road, Belle Vue Aces tackle Southampton at Speedway featuring the immortal Peter Craven. Stock Car Racing has equal prominence on the poster. It is hardly surprising that a Salford bus is caught passing along Chapel Street. A large number of services passed along this stretch of road at the time.   **25th JULY 1961 ● A.C. GILBERT**

Wagons originating mainly from the Southern and North Eastern Regions occupy the east end of the New Bailey Yard. Capstans and cobblestones dominate the foreground whilst the tight radius of lines within the yard can be appreciated here. The gable end of the Goods Forwarding Shed is on the left, behind which are the canopies of Salford Station. The approach road lay immediately behind the double gate but the prominent station signage above on the bridge parapet had disappeared shortly after Nationalisation. Walker and Homfray's Brewery Ltd off Eccles New Road also disappeared, closing on 28th February 1953 as part of the merger with Wilson's Brewery, Newton Heath. Note the four aspect colour light signals installed in 1928.   **c.1930 ● SALFORD LOCAL HISTORY LIBRARY**

BRAKE VAN TOUR

An enthusiasts Brake Van Tour of the Salford area, including a trip down the New Barns Branch, was organised by the North West Branch of the LCGB. No **51232** was the last remaining 'Pug' left in regular service and is standing at the head of its five van train in the bottom yard, also known as the 'Preston' Yard. Stanley Street lies immediately behind the wall. The veteran of 1891, which had been spruced up at Agecroft shed for the occasion, was ably supported by Jinty 0-6-0T No **47428** at the rear. After the tour, both locos returned to work the Irwell Street Goods Yards as usual the following Monday morning, and continued to do so for a further seven months until tragedy struck.

10th NOVEMBER 1962 ●
ALLAN SOMMERFIELD COLLECTION

On 28th May 1963, No 51232 broke an axle and was condemned on the spot. Kitson 'Dock Shunter' 0-4-0T No 47001 was hastily commandeered from Bank Hall before No **D2866**, a diesel shunter built by Yorkshire Engine Co. arrived on a more permanent basis. The chimney and cab of the 'Pug' are just visible standing behind a wagon at the now redundant coal stage. D2866 goes about her duties and has just passed under the four track viaduct carrying the ex-LNWR line. The area bounded by this and the Windsor Bridge line within Salford Goods was known as 'The Field'. Two large sheds were originally situated here to handle paper, cloth & flour which was an indication of the diversity of produce handled within the yard. The travelling crane also operated from within the site. Amongst the debris taking shelter under the viaduct are what appear to be two tar wagons and an old 36 gallon beer barrel.

23rd JULY 1963 ● **GRAHAM WHITEHEAD**

After languishing for over two months, No **51232** is awaiting its final journey to Horwich. The diminutive 'Pug' stands on a Flatrol well wagon supported by pallets. The wagon is capable of withstanding up to 40 tons in weight and can easily accommodate the 23 ton locomotive. Although it had been the last active member at work in Salford, two others still remained in service. No 51253 was transferred from Bank Hall, Liverpool across the city to Speke Junction in June 1963 to cover for a diesel shunter working at a nearby factory. It was also withdrawn in July 1963. This left No 51218 which had been in store at Bristol Barrow Road but was moved to Swansea East Dock to act as standby for former Cardiff Railway 0-4-0 Saddle Tank No 1338. It was eventually withdrawn from Neath (87A) in October 1964 Both these locos now survive in preservation.

8th AUGUST 1963 ● **GRAHAM WHITEHEAD**

Another aeriel view showing the complexity of railway goods yards, goods sheds and warehouses that once clustered around the viaducts carrying the ex-L&Y and LNW lines out of the city. The close proximity of the River Irwell, which formed the city boundary, also features prominently. Heavy air raids during World War Two over Manchester and Salford took their toll on the night of 22nd December 1940 when many buildings were destroyed. The railway network was a prime target and the stations at Mayfield and Manchester Exchange suffered serious damage. Salford Low Level Goods Yard was subjected to incendiary devices and the New Bailey Goods Shed was completely destroyed by fire - a smaller replacement shed was built post war. The viaduct carrying the LNWR lines was also breached at a point near the bottom of the incline from Oldfield Road, but this was quickly restored. The aftermath resulted in the yards and facilities going into slow decline bringing about the eventual closure of the New Bailey site on 23rd March 1964 and the remainder in August 1968.   **1930 ● A.W. HOBART**

1 - Albert Bridge
2 - Bridge Street
3 - River Irwell
4 - Irwell Street
5 - Quay Street
6 - Ralli Bros
7 - Stanley Street
8 - Sheet Shed
9 - Old Cloth Shed
10 - Paper Shed
11 - Coal Stage (behind viaduct)
12 - Preston Yard
13 - Part of 'The Field'
14 - LNWR lines to Ordsall Lane
15 - Carriage Sidings
16 - L&YR Lines
17 - Brown Brothers
18 - Salford Station
19 - New Bailey Street Goods Warehouse
20 - New Bailey Street
21 - Goods Office

HOPE STREET ENGINE SHED

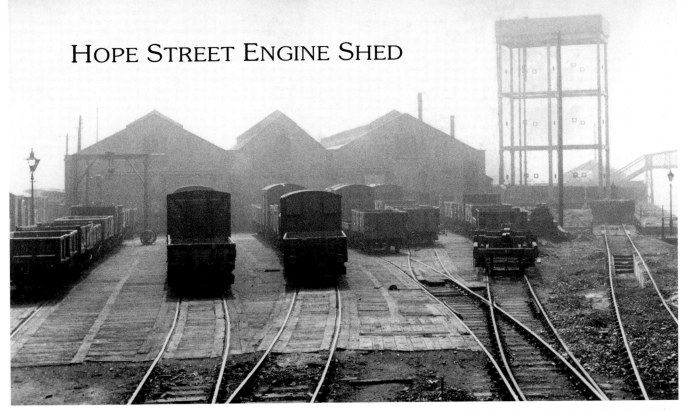

In 1871 the L&YR built a new eight road brick-built engine shed with a slated, triple gabled roof on land adjoining Windsor Bridge Cattle Station. Facilities included a 50ft turntable, inspection pits and a coal stage. The premises replaced three hopelessly cramped sheds which existed in the immediate vicinity. A two road building at Oldfield Road, constructed by the Manchester, Bolton & Bury Canal and Railway Company in 1844 was absorbed by the L&Y three years later. A three road shed, also known as Hope Street, was built by the East Lancs Railway in 1856 who also had another building on the opposite side of the line west of Oldfield Road. Hope Street *(also referred to as Windsor Bridge)* Shed closed upon the opening of Agecroft in 1889, although a servicing facility was retained throughout the L&Y period. This photograph, taken in the mid-1930's, shows the original building which had since become a wagon repair depot and as such outlived the days of steam. The turntable and pit remain in-situ whilst to the right, the New Barns branch descends to Manchester Docks.

c1935 ● W.A. CAMWELL

Two fascinating studies within the Hope Street building. The forges would almost certainly have been installed at the time the building was converted for wagon repairs. The museum piece is a solid metal wheel cart which is of rivetted construction and no doubt originates from the L&Y era.

c1966 ● BERNARD CRICK

One of the smaller signalboxes on the L&Y system was this specimen at Hope Street. The twelve lever box remained open from 1899 until 6th June 1964, at which time the sidings of the same name also ceased to function. The roof of the former Hope Street engine shed is prominent in the background as are the gasholders belonging to the Liverpool Road Gasworks.

**28th FEBRUARY 1963 ●
GRAHAM WHITEHEAD**

WINDSOR BRIDGE JUNCTION

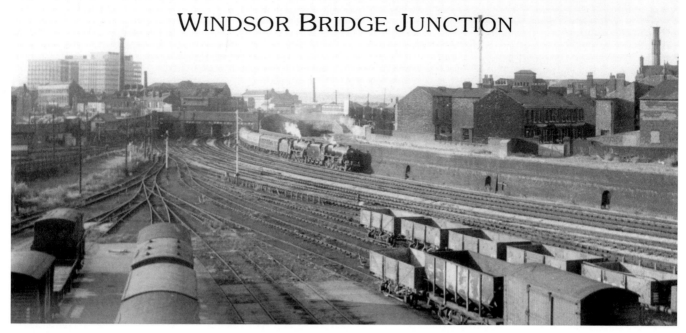

BR's last official main line steam working, the famous *15 Guinea Special* took place on Sunday, August 11th 1968. Stanier Class Five No 45110 worked the first and last leg of the railtour from Liverpool Lime Street to Manchester Victoria and return later in the day. Britannia Pacific No 70013 *Oliver Cromwell* took the train forward from Manchester Victoria to Carlisle via Bolton, Blackburn, Hellifield and the Settle and Carlisle route. The train then returned to Manchester double headed by a pair of Stanier Class Fives, Nos **44871** and **44781**. Oliver Cromwell returned light engine following the train. Viewed from a position on the former L&Y Hope Street engine shed roof, the Class Fives have just passed under Windsor Bridge and are nearing the end of the third leg of the journey after which No 45110 will return to Liverpool, appropriately traversing much of the former Liverpool and Manchester Railway route. Deep shadows from the pilot loco are cast against the retaining wall which was built in conjunction with the re-directed Manchester, Bolton and Bury Canal. Of the four locomotives involved, three survive in preservation but No 44781 was tragically cut up by R.A. King of Norwich at Bartlow near Haverhill after being wrecked in filming the 'Virgin Soldiers' for Columbia Pictures.   **11th AUGUST 1968 ● PAUL SHACKCLOTH**

No 47165, a Fowler designed 0-6-0 Dock Tank came from Fleetwood to test for suitability at Irwell Street. It was unable to negotiate the sharp curves and within a month had moved on to Bolton. Taken from a passing train, it is caught returning to Agecroft shed in the company of 'Pug' 0-4-0ST No **51232**.

OCTOBER 1961 ● SALFORD LOCAL HISTORY LIBRARY

Ex-L&Y 0-6-0ST No 51413 is engaged on shunting duties at Hope Street Yard, a regular turn for this loco or No 51496.

28th OCTOBER 1960 ● PETER FITTON

Hope Street Sidings and former engine shed fell victim to closure then wholesale demolition in the area which eventually cleared a path for the 'Windsor Link', a new line constructed between Windsor Bridge Junction on the former L&Y and Ordsall Lane Junction on the former LNWR. This provided a much needed north to south route through the city. A 350bhp 0-6-0 Diesel Shunter is engaged in the goods yard whilst a loaded flat wagon stands on ground once occupied by the New Barns branch.

1972 ● SALFORD LOCAL HISTORY LIBRARY

THE L&Y SALFORD DOCKS BRANCH

The L&Y obtained powers in 1890 to construct a branch from Windsor Bridge to a site between No 8 Dock and Manchester Racecourse offering connections with lines being constructed by the Manchester Ship Canal Company. The double track railway to New Barns Junction opened on 28th March 1898, shortly after which a station named New Barns was opened specifically for race traffic. The racecourse occupied land bound by the River Irwell and Broadway and was known as the New Barns Estate. At the turn of the century, the Ship Canal Company proposed to extend their facilities by the construction of a new dock on the site. As a consequence, the last race meeting took place on 1st November 1901 after which excavation and construction began in earnest. The new No 9 Dock was formally declared open by King Edward VII and Queen Alexandra on 13th July 1905. The proceeds from the sale of the land allowed the company to develop a new racecourse, once more at Castle Irwell. New Barns Station served racegoers for a mere four years after which it became commonly known as the 'Docks Station'. It was used by the workforce until 1939 but neither train or station ever appeared in the public timetable. In addition, the 'Salford Docks Mission' organised annual childrens' outings to the Fylde coast whilst records also show that evacuees left from there. After the war it fell into disrepair, although the station building was still in use at the end of the steam era, acting as a mission hall. The line was fraught with problems and because of the steep gradient, the signalman at New Barns Junction Signalbox could not allow trains to leave until there was a clear path on to the main line beyond Windsor Bridge Junction. In the early days, trains were invariably assisted by the 'Little Egberts' - L&Y 0-8-2 Banking Tanks introduced in 1904 and Nos 1504/5 were allocated to Agecroft specifically for the purpose. After their withdrawal in 1929, the LMS 'Austin Seven' 0-8-0's appeared. Six-coupled diesel shunters were present when the line finally closed on 15th June 1963.

After passing Hope Street Engine Shed on a falling gradient of 1 in 47, the branch entered the 471 yard West Egerton Street tunnel, passing under the former LNWR lines west of Ordsall Lane station. It then passed through Ellesmere Street (291 yards) and West Park Street (172 yards) tunnels before going beneath the MSC Railway to connect with a branch of this at New Barns Junction. A line once passed through the derelict single tunnel archway to serve both the Liverpool Road Brick and Gas Works, crossing the road on the level. The high level footbridge in view connects Harrogate Street and Hope Street.

24th MARCH 1962 ● G. HARROP

The original New Barns (later Docks) Station Booking Office standing on Hulton Street. A single platform on a gradient of 1 in 68 lay just beyond West Park Street Tunnel, access to which was down a long flight of steps.

24th MARCH 1962 ● G. HARROP

The neck of the 1.5 mile branch. The Manchester Ship Canal line passes overhead and the extensive Exchange Sidings lie ahead. An engine shed belonging to the MSC occupied a part of the site here. No 8 Dock is in the background behind New Barns Junction Signalbox, a traditional L&Y structure with brick base and 40 lever frame.

24th MARCH 1962 ● G. HARROP

WINDSOR BRIDGE

Stanier Class Five No 44767, the only member of the 842 strong class to be fitted with outside Stephenson link motion, picks up speed after clearing Salford Station with a Down Southport express. The loco had been at Bank Hall throughout the 1950's but enjoyed a brief sojourn at Southport from March 1962 until November 1964. It happily survives in preservation and now carries nameplates *'George Stephenson'*.

17th SEPTEMBER 1963 ●
R.W. MILLER COLLECTION

Beyond Windsor Bridge, the ex-L&Y main lines diverge. The direct line to Agecroft Junction via Pendleton (Old) is behind the newly installed fogsignalman's hut, a local product of Newton Heath Works which would have replaced an earlier wooden one. The 'Fogging Post' as it was known, contained a small coal stove and wooden locker to sit on. Outside was the detonator placing machine and a wooden cupboard which would contain the miniature signal arm repeaters for the associated distant arms mounted on the bracket signals. The running lines in the foreground are the Up and Down Fast and Up and Down Slow which pass through Pendleton (Broad Street) whilst the line serving the New Barns Branch trails in on the right. Newton Heath Class Five No **44818** is running light engine on the Down Slow, possibly on its way to Agecroft shed for servicing. An impressive array of semaphore signals remain present in this view looking East. Windsor Bridge No 3 signalbox is visible in the right background, beyond which are the original Salford University buildings standing on The Crescent.   **1967** ● **E.F. BENTLEY**

AEC Reliance No 102 crosses Allwood Street bridge on Oldfield Road, en-route to Peel Green on Service 5 and is about to pass the 'Kings Arms', a typical Salford corner pub. The licensee of this Wilsons house would have doubtless enjoyed commanding views from the upstairs windows on Allwood Street directly on to the railway. In vision would be Oldfield Road Signalboxes Nos 1 and 2 controlling the Fast and Slow lines between Salford Station and Windsor Bridge, Oldfield Road Sidings and traffic in and out of Irwell Street goods via the incline. Additionally, Oldfield Road Coal stage and a number of associated railway cabins were on site. The Manchester, Bury and Bolton Canal also passed under both railway and bridge at this point.

26th OCTOBER 1967 ● **P.J. THOMPSON**

OLDFIELD ROAD

THE CRESCENT

The old Technical College building dominates the scene here. Situated within Peel Park, it was threatened with demolition in 1961 but happily survived to become part of the University campus. Salford Daimler CVG6 No **484**, having already crossed Windsor Bridge, moves on to The Crescent heading towards Victoria Bus Station on Service 25. This was another of the distinctive 'circular' routes operating within the city - running between Victoria and Lancaster Road/Swinton Park Road, travelling outward via Weaste and returning via Pendleton. Service 30 ran in the opposite direction. A similar bus, No **430** on Service 27 follows in its path. The Commer Karrier goods wagon passing by was a typical sight on Salford's busy main roads at this time. A municipal weighing machine was installed on the south side of the roadway at Windsor Bridge in May 1956 and was considered to be one of the largest in the country.   **26th OCTOBER 1967** ● **P.J. THOMPSON**

This distinctive green Salford bus stop offered the travelling public more information than its Manchester counterpart which showed service numbers only at best. This one is on Chapel Street opposite the junction with Statham Street which also acted as a fare stage for routes via Bolton Road only. Services 19 & 21, coupled with the cross-city 57 & 77's, were short workings, operating early mornings only - Monday to Saturday - from King Street West to Swinton & Pendlebury, returning as far as Bridge Street. Similarly, Service 42 worked to Swinton Park Road via Broad Street & Bolton Road, returning the same way. No 29 was a night service only. Daimler CVG6 No **128** is on Service 56 to Piccadilly in this view looking towards Frederick Road. The imposing building opposite was purpose built as a funeral parlour by Coops & Sons Ltd. in 1900. They were one of the most well known businesses in a city which was one of the unhealthiest places to live in Britain in the second half of the 19th century. An unusual feature was that horses were once stabled on the first floor, access being by means of a ramp. The Pendleton Co-operative Society took over in 1955.   **22nd MARCH 1969** ● **P.J. THOMPSON**

BROAD STREET

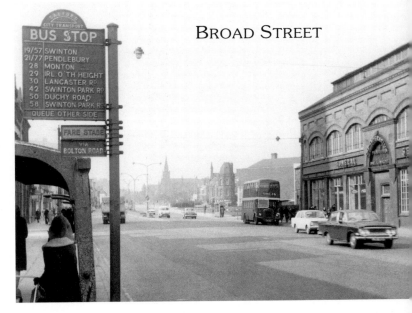

CROSS LANE

The traction pole removal gang are busy at work on Cross Lane, near the site of the former Salford Cattle Market between Unwin Street and West High Street, which was founded as early as 1774. The poles were a legacy of the conventional tramway era in Salford - which had ended 22 years earlier in 1947. The lighting wire insulating bracket at the top of the pole is one of the common variety. The Daimler CVG6 bus, No **543**, is working back to Manchester on Service 84 and passing along a once thriving thoroughfare, renowned for its numerous public houses. During the 1950's, Salford had more licensed premises per head of population than any other city in Great Britain. Further down Cross Lane and lying submerged beneath the tarmacadam was the tramway junction with Regent Road, known as a 'Grand Union'. This has since been removed and transported to Crich National Tramway Museum for re-assembly as a display item, being one of the largest in Great Britain. It has two lines around each of the four corners and two across in every direction.   **7th JUNE 1969 ● P.J. THOMPSON**

DRIVER TRAINING BUS

BBA 560 is a noteworthy vehicle. Introduced in 1939 as fleet number 235, the AEC Regent has Park Royal bodywork and is seen standing at Monton Green. Two buses, Nos 234 and 235 were converted to dual-control driving instruction vehicles in 1948, being re-numbered 97 and **98** respectively in 1950. The second steering wheel is visible through the window immediately behind the cab. Note also the second off-side mirror. No 97 was sold for scrap in 1970, but No 98 was preserved by Roy Marshall and, after a period of storage at Frederick Road, was splendidly restored to its original 1939 condition. It is now part of the collection at the Manchester Museum of Transport and took a prominent part in the 'Salford 100' event staged there in October 2003.   **c.1960 ● DAVID YOUNG COLLECTION**

The crew of bus No 105 have summoned assistance at Windsor Bridge triangle from nearby Frederick Road depot. The van in attendance was numbered **C3** (GBA 3), a Morris Commercial new in 1952. Salford's fleet of supplementary non-PSV vehicles over the years was a complex one. There were numerous variations and conversions from 1907 onwards including tower wagons and steam lorries etc. C3 (and sister C2) seemed to have been classed as light repair vans, sent out to attend to minor incidents such as this, when the tow wagon was not required. C5 and C6 were classed as 'goods vans' and the fleet further extended to C16 which included shooting brakes, tipper wagons, estate cars and a mobile canteen. The bus was on a part day extra service (possibly going to Hope Hospital), the passengers having already transferred to another vehicle.

1954 ● E. GRAY

The view towards Manchester from the Broad Street platforms serving the Fast lines, which shows the crossover connecting with the Up and Down slow. Pendleton Broad Street and the 28 lever station signalbox opened on 13th June 1887 after the L&Y had obtained powers to build a new line from Windsor Bridge to Swinton. A Salford Leyland bus crosses the railway on Frederick Road, possibly returning to the garage which was situated nearby, immediately west of the River Irwell near Wallness Bridge.

c.1960 ● ROBERT HUMM COLLECTION

Broad Street Station, or 'New' as it was so often called, was situated at the junction of Ford Lane and Broughton Road. The building was a modest affair but the facilities were almost palatial compared to those at the 'Old' station, a short distance down Broughton Road on the other side *(see page 86)*. Local passenger services between Wigan Wallgate and Manchester Victoria accounted for much of the traffic but the *Summer Timetable of 1958* reveals that three Blackpool trains also called here, first stop out of Victoria, which avoided the inconvenience of locals having to first get into the city. They were:

WEEKDAYS 8.50amSX to Blackpool Central
8.55amSO to Blackpool Central
10.45amSO to Blackpool Central

SUNDAYS 6.04am to Blackpool Central
8.46am to Blackpool Central
9.55am to Blackpool North & Central

JUNE 1968 ● GORDON COLTAS

PENDLETON BROAD STREET

The short, intermittent Service 34 could perhaps best be described as a low profile route - running largely along the back streets of Pendleton and Charlestown. It officially operated between Regent Bridge or Pendleton Church and Langley Road at the junction of Agecroft Road, via Cromwell Road and Whit Lane. No **277**, An AEC Regent III introduced in 1947, is standing in Gloucester Street - the terminus for Pendleton Church and situated between Pendleton 'New' and 'Old' Stations. The bus service offered no connection with the local train timetables but was convenient for mourners visiting the Salford Northern Cemetery on Agecroft Road.

5th AUGUST 1959 ● P.J. THOMPSON

The first two bays of Frederick Road Tramway Depot were ready by September 1901 to coincide with the arrival of the first electric cars. When complete the depot could accommodate 180 cars on 20 tracks, 15 of which were equipped with inspection pits. An imposing entrance arch *(still in situ - courtesy of a preservation order)* and further extensions were added in 1907, but by that time, the red brick built car shed with stone dressing was generally considered to be one of the finest of its type in the country. By 1937 the allocation was 137 trams, 39 buses and 17 ancillary vehicles. Eleven years after the demise of the tram, No **346**, a Daimler CVD6 of 1948 with Metro-Cammell bodywork and one of a batch originally ordered by Chester Corporation, is standing inside the garage. They were deemed surplus to requirements and Chief Executive Charles Baroth quickly diverted them to Salford instead. A similar vehicle, No 343 carried an oval plate lettered 'GB' at the rear below the fleet number, as this new bus travelled to Copenhagen for the 1948 British Exhibition held there, crewed by Frederick Road men. After its return to the UK, the bus carried a commemorative plaque in the lower saloon whilst retaining the oval plate in ordinary service.

MAY 1958 ● J. FOZARD

An interesting parade has been assembled in the yard of Frederick Road Depot on the occasion of an Omnibus Society visit. Standing at the head, in front of two of the eight archways offering entrance is No **451**, a Daimler CVG6 with Burlingham 22 seat bodywork. Carrying primrose livery, it acted as the City Transport Committee's coach between 1951 and 1962 - but in reality saw very little service. It was replaced by No 101, an AEC Reliance with Fanfare 26-seat coach bodywork. Alongside is another single deck, No **450** - a Daimler CVG6/Burlingham followed by No **108** *(formerly No 28)* - a 1934 Leyland TD3 with 1949 Burlingham body, instead of the original Massey body. The fourth bus in view is No **261**, a 1947 Crossley DD42/3 with Metro-Cammell bodywork. In February 1952, Salford had 304 buses in service operated by a staff of 1,571 men and women including administration and servicing.

22nd JULY 1951 ● ROY MARSHALL

A pair of consecutively numbered buses, fleet numbers **258** and **259** stand over the pits in Frederick Road Works. They are Metro-Cammell bodied Crossley DD42/3 vehicles, introduced in 1947 and withdrawn from service in the early 1960's. By 1938, buses had begun to take over that portion of the depot nearest Frederick Road, as many trams had been withdrawn by then. The remaining cars were restricted to 10 tracks inside the depot served by a traverser running across the end of the tracks, but after the final withdrawal of the trams in 1947, the traverser pit was filled in.

AUGUST 1957 ● R. MACK

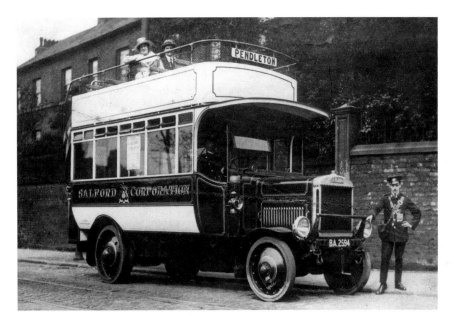

SALFORD'S FIRST BUS

BA 2594 was Salford's first bus, fleet No **1.** It was a Leyland 31M, with Leyland bodywork and was introduced into service on 5th July 1920. The early operation was between Pendleton Office and Great Cheetham Street, mainly along roads which had not enjoyed a public service before. This inter-suburban route was developed into the well-known Service 1 of later years, running between Weaste and Mandley Park. The vehicle was converted into a Tower Wagon in 1928 and given a new fleet number - 404, but was subsequently sold on to Derby Corporation in October 1947.

1920 ● A. HAYNES COLLECTION

Passing St. Thomas's Church, Pendleton is No 168, a Leyland PD2/40 with Metro-Cammell bodywork introduced in 1963. It is working on Service 12, Bolton to Greengate, via Little Hulton, Walkden, Roe Green, Worsley and Pendleton. Although Greengate was in Salford, buses terminating there displayed 'Manchester', which was probably more appropriate for the longer-distance services such as No 12, even if not strictly accurate. Behind No 168 is a Lancashire United single-deck bus displaying Service 41 - Eccles. This again ran from Bolton but via Farnworth, Walkden, Worsley and Barton Bridge to Eccles. As the route passed under the Bridgewater Canal, single deck vehicles were necessary. The vehicle appears to be one of only three Leyland Tiger PSUC1's with Duple Bodywork built in 1966 which carried Fleet Nos 211-3. The premises of Milford-Astor, seen between bus and church, were ravaged by fire in the early 1970's and subsequently demolished.

c1968 ● DAVID YOUNG COLLECTION

Passing in the opposite direction is Daimler CVG6 No 4034, now carrying the post-1969 SELNEC livery of sunglow orange and white, was formerly Salford No 145. The bus is on Service 56, which at this time ran between Manchester Piccadilly and Pendlebury. The destination blind is misleading as the bus is travelling *from* Piccadilly heading north west on Broad Street.

**c1970 ●
DAVID YOUNG COLLECTION**

Forging up the bank away from Pendleton on the Fast Line is Stanier Class Five No **45151.** This loco isn't a Newton Heath or Blackpool example as one might expect, but hails from Motherwell (66B) - a rare bird indeed! In all probability it has been borrowed by Newton Heath after having arrived on a working from either Carlisle or Glasgow. If so, either Kingmoor or Polmadie had done the same. Motherwell certainly had no diagrams to the Manchester area. Scottish based Class Fives carried '5MT' on their cab sides above the number, rather than the usual '5' and those shopped at St. Rollox also carried the larger cab side numerals. The heavy concentration of industry in the Pendleton area is obvious with no fewer than eleven factory chimneys in view. Engineering and textiles were the prominent areas of activity.

3rd JULY 1961 ● W.D. COOPER

IRLAM
THE FAST LINES

A Blackpool express at the same location has a more familiar member in charge. No **44730**, a Blackpool stalwart, was a regular performer throughout the 1950's and early 60's, handling the intensive Blackpool to Manchester Victoria service. Few problems were encountered by the enginemen there and at the time of the photograph, a stud of eighteen Stanier Class Five 4-6-0's were kept in first class mechanical condition. Irlam Signalbox, standing between the Fast and Slow lines, can be seen on the right. This small ex-L&Y box had 36 levers and closed before the end of steam on 19th December 1967.

28th MAY 1963 ● W.D. COOPER

BRINDLE HEATH DOWN SIDINGS

A fascinating glimpse of Brindle Heath Down Sidings during the LMS period. Sleeper fencing (ex-L&Y) protects the yard which contains an interesting assortment of wagons. A cattle van originating from the Southern Region stands sandwiched between a number of plank wagons, one of which still carries the earlier L&Y lettering. There are also a number of private owner examples lurking in the background. Affixed to the gate is a standard London, Midland and Scottish Railway Warning Sign, emphasising that sidings are private property. The period gas lamp is conveniently sited to illuminate the entrance at night.

20th APRIL 1933 ● **SALFORD LOCAL HISTORY LIBRARY**

A stopping train from Manchester Victoria to Bolton is about to pass under the flyover carrying the Fast Lines towards Pendlebury. Having called at Pendleton Broad Street, Stanier Class 4 2-6-4T No **42647** has the Brindle Heath Junction home splitting signal in its favour, and will shortly pass Agecroft shed on the Connecting Line on its way to Agecroft Junction. A number of trains were routed this way rather than using the original line via Pendleton (Old) Station. Brindle Heath Down Sidings Signalbox is visible and in its latter years was opened only as required, depending on the seasonal flow or declining traffic.

12th AUGUST 1960 ● **W.D. COOPER**

August Bank Holiday Monday during the 1950's and early 60's was a particularly busy day for BR. All manner of excursion trains were organised, travelling mainly to the coast, and this trio of Class Fives are involved in such activities. No **45195** (26B) takes the Fast Line, no doubt on its way to Blackpool, whilst Nos **44906** (8A) and **45019** (8F) have reversed on to their empty stock in the holding sidings (or loops) opposite Brindle Heath Down Sidings, after having been drawn out of Irlam Carriage Shed by a pilot loco. The reporting numbers carried by these two are consecutive - 1Z32 and 1Z33, which indicated inter-regional trains. **28th AUGUST 1961** ● **W.D. COOPER**

THE IRLAM LOOPS

BRINDLE HEATH UP SIDINGS

Agecroft Crab 2-6-0 No 42724 makes a smoky exit from Brindle Heath Up Sidings with a train of empty wagons. It is about to pass under the flyover carrying the Fast Lines to Pendlebury and Wigan. The Slow Lines trail in above the engine whilst through the array of semaphores, a 2-6-4 Stanier tank is on the Connecting Line to Agecroft Junction, possibly coming on shed. The wagon capacity for the Down Sidings was between 800 and 1,000 and a similar number could be accommodated in the Up Sidings. In addition, Brindle Heath Old Sidings, between Pendleton 'Old' Station and Agecroft Junction, could handle a further 300 to 600 wagons. **13th APRIL 1962 ● W.D. COOPER**

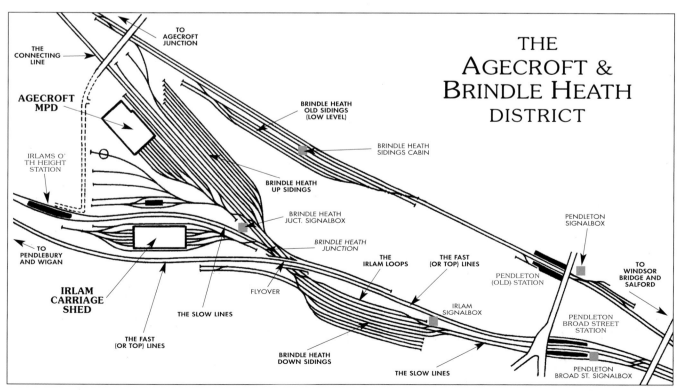

THE AGECROFT & BRINDLE HEATH DISTRICT

BRINDLE HEATH JUNCTION

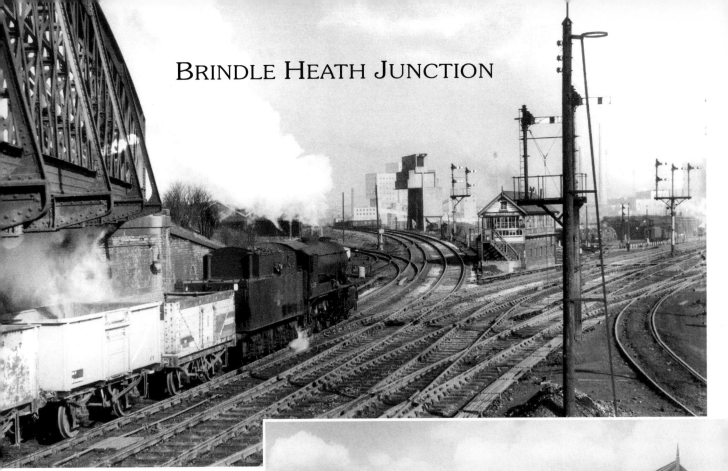

WD 2-8-0 No 90359 passes under the flyover carrying the Fast Lines and takes the Slow Line at the foot of Pendlebury Bank with empty mineral wagons. Agecroft shed yard is visible beyond Brindle Heath Junction Signalbox.

13th APRIL 1962 ● W.D. COOPER

Travelling in the opposite direction is Stanier 2-6-4T No **42570** with a stopping train to Manchester Victoria.

9th JULY 1960 ● W.D. COOPER

GT3

Gas Turbine No GT3 awaits cutting up in the scrapyard of Thomas Ward Ltd., situated beyond Brindle Heath Down Sidings. The only BR locos cut up here were ex-L&Y 'A' Class Nos 52120 and 52360 in May 1959, but a number of industrial and private locos were dealt with. The yard closed in 1982.

27th FEBRUARY 1966 ●
A.C. GILBERT

An experimental Gas Turbine 4-6-0 No GT3 emerged from Vulcan Foundry early in 1961. It was built as a private venture by the Gas Turbine Division of English Electric whilst British Railways provided the facilities for exhaustive trials. The locomotive, designed by Mr. J.O.P. Hughes, was the culmination of 15 years' work. Trials at Rugby Testing Station were followed by trips over the former Great Central line between Leicester and Marylebone and the Crewe - Carlisle section of the West Coast Main Line. Although GT3 performed creditably, its introduction coincided with an ever increasing fleet of diesel locomotives which were becoming popular. This handsome machine was oil-fired and had mechanical transmission with a conventional 4-6-0 wheel arrangement. A corridor passed through the tender which housed oil fuel tanks on either side. Its livery was an unusual combination - light brown set off with dark green and orange bands. After trials it faded into obscurity, being considered an uneconomic proposition, a major disadvantage being its reversing mechanism. GT3 returned to Vulcan Foundry where the turbine plant was stripped out. The remains were sold to Thomas Ward for scrap and arrived there behind Standard Class 4 4-6-0 No 75032.

Aspinall developed a powerful shunting engine in 1897 with Belpaire boiler and push-pull regulator. The class of twenty were known as 'Rapid Shunting Engines', and this example, No **494**, certainly lived up to its name. Problems with this type of regulator had often been recorded and on this occasion it had not been properly closed, resulting in the loco running away off shed before coming to grief at the end of the yard. The buffer stops offered only token resistance and Brindle Heath Junction Signalbox took the full brunt of the force, resulting in considerable structural damage as can be seen. Enginemen and signalmen pose for the camera in time honoured fashion, but serious operating difficulties in the area became a problem. Several other minor mishaps occurred before the troublesome regulators were replaced at Horwich Works by those of a standard type. The wooden structure in front of the signalbox was the toilet facility.

1910 ● SALFORD LOCAL HISTORY LIBRARY

The rebuilt box in BR days looking east towards Pendleton. Brindle Heath Down Siding Signalbox is visible through the flyover. The Junction box was originally constructed in 1899 with the opening of Agecroft shed. Note the unusual abbreviation for 'Junction' on the end of the box.

c.1968 ● ALLAN SOMMERFIELD

No 45154 - *Lanarkshire Yeomanry,* one of only four Stanier Class Fives to receive names, is in charge of a day excursion to Blackpool with non-corridor stock and is about to attack Pendlebury Bank.

9th JULY 1960 ● W.D. COOPER

A GLIMPSE OF
L&Y LOCOS
AT WORK

Aspinall locomotives in tandem. The practice of double heading trains in L&Y days was unusual and on this occasion the pilot is one of the 7ft 3in 4-4-0 Passenger engines built in 1891 whilst behind is a member of the celebrated 'Highflyer' 4-4-2 Class. They are descending Pendlebury Bank on the Fast (or top) Line with a heavy Manchester bound train. The track in the foreground is the headshunt of Irlam Carriage Sidings where there is evidence that more than one fire has been thrown out. Note the bushes planted at regular intervals in order to aid the stabilisation of the bank. Irlams o' th' Height Home Starter signal is off, ready to accept a train on the Down Slow line.

c.1909 ● JOHN RYAN COLLECTION

An unidentified 'Dreadnought' 4-6-0 approaches Brindle Heath Junction with a returning test train from Blackpool Talbot Road *(see below)*. In the bottom right hand corner, a Hoy 0-8-0 Coal Engine can just be seen moving down the coal stage road at the back of Agecroft shed. On the horizon stands Agecroft Colliery which, at the time, was the property of Manchester Collieries Ltd. It first closed in 1932 but twenty years later, after Nationalisation, the NCB reopened it and rebuilt two of the original pits, whilst a new shaft was also sunk. New sidings had been laid and by 1960, two conveyor belts were in operation connecting the pit head to a bunker for coal wagons and to the coal handling plant in the adjacent power station sidings.

c.1922 ● JOHN RYAN COLLECTION

The same loco on the outward journey approaching Irlams o' th' Height Station and attacking the Pendlebury Bank Slow Line. Between 1920 and 1924, various test runs were made between Manchester Victoria and Blackpool Talbot Road. The trains always ran on Sundays to ensure a clear road ahead and involved loads of up to 18 carriages representing over 450 tons behind the tender. The trials involved 4-6-0 locos of both L&Y and LNW origin. The 'Dreadnought', 'Prince of Wales' and 'Claughton' were the classes represented and although the results proved inconclusive, all three apparently acquitted themselves well.

c.1922 ● JOHN RYAN COLLECTION

A dramatic increase in traffic on the L&Y in the Salford area during the 1870-80 period resulted in the development of a new engine shed and facilities at Agecroft. A dead end building containing 8 roads was built to house 48 locomotives and was erected in 1889 under the direction of Aspinall. A Northlight roof, coal hole with water tank over and a 50ft turntable were standard features - as was the foreman's bay window which offered views of the shed yard and the clock over the timekeeper's office. Engines were transferred from the existing, restricted site at Hope Street, near Windsor Bridge on completion and in 1901, the shed further benefited from the installation of a wheel drop, by which time the allocation was approaching 100 with most L&Y classes represented. The shed was coded No 13 from the outset and engines outstationed at Hull and York came under its supervision for 12 years prior to the Grouping. From December 1930, a prefix 'C' was added to the code and enamel plates began to appear on the smokebox door. This was in reference to the newly created Central Division of the LMS which had, in turn, succeeded the Western 'B' Division. After further reorganisation in 1935, it became 26B and under the wings of Newton Heath. A final change to 9J during the BR period on 9th September 1963 was brought about by the merger of the former Manchester Districts of Longsight and Newton Heath. The shed closed on 22nd October 1966, hastened by problems of local mining subsidence, and the allocation of 32 locos were dispersed. This evocative early view shows all 8 roads, the foreman's bay window, and a small selection of motive power. The four L&Y water columns remained present throughout the shed's existence but the gas lamps were replaced by electric lighting over each road on the shed roof during the LMS period. **c.1912 ● ALLAN SOMMERFIELD COLLECTION**

Another view of the immaculate shed yard showing the close proximity of Brindle Heath Down Sidings. Agecroft covered a diverse range of work - from the diminutive 0-4-0 'Pugs' shunting at Irwell Street Goods yard to the mighty 4-6-0 'Dreadnoughts', which handled the Manchester to York expresses. **c.1912 ● ALLAN SOMMERFIELD COLLECTION**

A pair of 'Little Egberts', Nos 1503/4 are positioned on the newly installed 70ft turntable for balancing purposes. The 0-8-2 tank engines, which operated on the 'New Barns Branch' to the docks, had already been withdrawn from service. **c.1912 ● ALLAN SOMMERFIELD COLLECTION**

L&Y GALLERY

Barton Wright 0-6-2T No 223 built by Dübs, entered service in December 1882 and was withdrawn in November 1910. The clock tower over the time office was a distinctive feature at Agecroft around the turn of the century.

c.1900 ● REAL PHOTOS

Aspinall 6' 0" 4-4-0 Passenger Tender Engine No 982 built by Beyer Peacock in August 1888 and rebuilt with Belpaire boiler in May 1915. This handsome engine was withdrawn in February 1932 carrying LMS No 10106.   c.1900 ● REAL PHOTOS

Aspinall Class 21 0-4-0ST 'Pug' No 68, Works No 811 and built at Horwich in October 1901. It became LMS No 11218 before BR No 51218 in April 1949. 57 of the diminutive 'Pug' Class were built in 6 lots between November 1891 and July 1910 under the direction of Aspinall, Hoy and Hughes. They principally worked the dock lines at Liverpool, Fleetwood and Goole as well as goods yards in the Manchester and Salford area. Newton Heath, Goole, Agecroft, Sandhills (Bank Hall), Aintree and Fleetwood sheds all had examples to call on. 23 members of the class survived Nationalisation by which time Bath, Bristol, Burton-on-Trent and Crewe South had been blessed by their presence. No 68 stands in the yard at Agecroft with Shedmaster Eric Mason on the footplate. The locomotive happily survives in preservation.

c.1920 ● JOHN G. HARTSHORNE COLLECTION

Aspinall Small Boilered 0-8-0 Tender Engine No 1452 is a visitor from Aintree. The loco entered service in September 1904 and was successfully converted to a four-cylinder compound in February 1906. It became LMS No 12760 before withdrawal in September 1926.

c.1920 ● E. MASON

In 1908/9, Agecroft received four members of the Aspinall 'Highflyer' 4-4-2 Class to work on the York services with a further three arriving in 1912 - but by 1921, they were reduced to No 1418 only. A visitor from Low Moor, **No 1423** drifts off the shed during the early LMS period.
20th DECEMBER 1924 ● PAUL SHACKCLOTH COLLECTION

The first 'Class 28' 0-6-0 to enter service was No 11, Works No 11, which emerged from Horwich Works on 12th September 1889. A further 82 engines went into service, all of which were either built with Belpaire fireboxes and super-heated boilers or converted from the original saturated type. No 11, which was dealt with in October 1914, stands in the shed yard near the coal hole. A recently renumbered 2-4-2 Radial tank, No **10810** is discernable stabled on shed in the background. **c.1924 ● JOHN G. HARTSHORNE COLLECTION**

An immaculate Hughes 'Dreadnought' 4-6-0 No 1509 stands at the throat of the shed yard. The three figures on the footplate are Driver Walter Trafford and Fireman Elisha Horrocks, accompanied by Shedmaster Eric Mason. **c.1920 ● REAL PHOTOS**

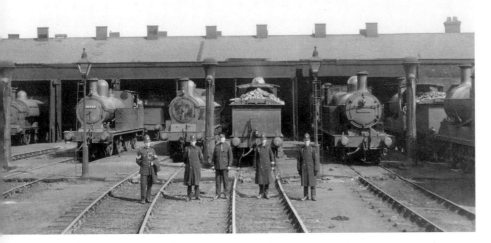

A view of the shed yard from the newly erected coaling plant, before the roof received attention. A cross section of typical motive power is present. The ex-L&Y are still strongly represented with three 'A' Class 0-6-0's, a pair of 'Radial' 2-4-2 Tanks and a large boilered 0-8-0. A 'Baltic' 4-6-4 Tank and two of the newer 'Crab' 2-6-0's are also present. The engine blowing off steam on number one road, nearest to the shedmaster's extended office is the prototype, No **13000**, which first appeared in LMS red livery on 23rd April 1926. This loco survives in preservation at the Barrow Hill Roundhouse, Staveley in its final BR condition numbered 42700.

1936 ● ALLAN SOMMERFIELD COLLECTION

Standing beside the coal stage are a pair of 'Baltic' 4-6-4 tanks, Nos **11110** and **11111**. These impressive looking locos were the last examples built with this wheel arrangement. They were adapted by Hughes from the four cylinder 4-6-0 'Dreadnought' Class and during 1924, ten members emerged from Horwich Works. They were found to be unsuitable for many of the Central Lines duties and, after being tried elsewhere, eg. on the Manchester London Road to Buxton line, they returned to their native haunts, working mainly out of Agecroft and Bolton sheds. No 11110, the first in service, was also the last, being withdrawn in January 1942.

c.1938 ● SALFORD LOCAL HISTORY LIBRARY

The 1926 National coal strike resulted in the local constabulary being assigned to protect the buildings at Agecroft against potential strike breakers. A sergeant, with a raincoat draped over his arm, may well have instructed the four officers to stand to attention as this was one of a series of official photographs taken at the time. The engines in view all appear to be out of steam and the only ones discernable are a pair of 'Radial' 2-4-2 tanks, Nos **10810** and **10894**, both Agecroft engines.

1926 ● ALLAN SOMMERFIELD COLLECTION

Whilst the LMS eventually invested in upgrading the facilities at many of the engine sheds they inherited, the breakdown trains and cranes were a different matter. By 1933, Agecroft had dispensed with the tool and travelling vans used during the L&Y period. The Tool Van, numbered 8, was a converted 6 wheel, 32 ft birdcage, 3 compartment passenger brake and the Travelling Van, numbered 41, was a converted 4 wheel, 27ft 6ins, birdcage passenger brake. The original 10 ton hand crane with straight jib, numbered 1197 and Safety Wagon No 315 are now sandwiched between a pair of ex-Midland Railway 6 wheel clerestories, suitably converted. The train engine is ex-L&Y 'A' Class 0-6-0 No **12283**.

30th JULY 1933 ● H.F. WHEELER

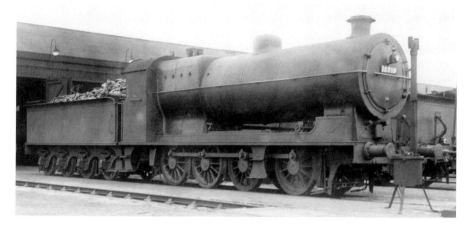

Large boilered 0-8-0 No 12919 (C13) rests between duties. Shortly after being built in September 1917, this loco, which was originally numbered 698, together with small boilered 0-8-0 No 715, were observed at work on the GWR at Pontypool Road early in 1918. According to Mason *(Lancashire and Yorkshire in the 20th Century)*, the Great Western men were impressed with the comfortable footplate and the loco's ability to pull big loads without being thrashed.

c.1930 ● PAUL SHACKCLOTH COLLECTION

Standing at the throat of Irlam Carriage Sidings is LNWR Whale 'Experiment' Class 4-6-0 No **830** *Phosphorus*. The photo may well have been taken during 1922, immediately prior to the Grouping, when the L&Y and LNWR amalgamated. The Slow Lines to Pendlebury lie between *Phosphorus* and a L&Y 'A' Class 0-6-0 coming on to the shed. A pair of 0-6-0 Saddle Tanks are at work within the Brindle Heath Down Sidings complex.

c.1922 ● A.G. ELLIS

VISITING LOCOMOTIVES

October 1930 marked the Centenary of the opening of the Liverpool and Manchester Railway. The occasion was marked by the staging of an exhibition at Wavertree, Liverpool, where an assortment of locomotives and rolling stock were assembled. This included the veteran *'Lion'*, which offered rides to the public on a circuit of track which had been specially laid. The 0-4-2 engine had been built by Todd, Kitson and Laird in 1838, specifically for the L&M. It was sold in 1859 to the Mersey Docks and Harbour Board for shunting duties after which it became a stationary engine. At the end of the proceedings, it was hastily decided that Manchester should have a 'piece of the action', and most of the exhibits were transferred there. The locos assembled at Agecroft for a 'wash and brush up' en-route before moving on (out of steam) to Victoria Station where two bay platforms had been made available. After the one day event, the locos returned to Agecroft late on Saturday evening for stabling prior to dispersal early the following week. Sunday afternoon presented a photographic opportunity to record the line up in the shed yard and some of Agecroft's inhabitants had been temporarily banished to Brindle Heath Sidings! The locos in view are Ex-L&Y Dreadnought 4-6-0 No **10452** (which wasn't part of the show), ex-GWR 4-6-0 No **6029 King Stephen,** ex-SR 4-6-0 No **850 Lord Nelson** and 0-4-2 *Lion.* Also present were Beyer Garratt No **4972**, LMR Royal Scot 4-6-0 No **6161 King's Own** and the 'Hush-Hush' engine, LNE four-cylinder compound 4-6-4 No **10000**. After the celebrations, *Lion* became a museum exhibit in Liverpool before achieving immortality, starring in the 1950's Ealing comedy 'The Titfield Thunderbolt'. She now resides at the Manchester Museum of Science and Industry.   **5th OCTOBER 1930 ● ALLAN SOMMERFIELD COLLECTION**

CARLISLE (UPPERBY)

BR Standard Class 7 Britannia Pacific No 70032, formerly ***Tennyson*** stands in light steam in the shed yard. In their heyday during the 1950's, the sighting of a 'Brit' on lowly Agecroft shed would have been almost unheard of. When the majority of the class gravitated to Carlisle in the mid-sixties, they became a common sight, working in with express freight, parcels and the occasional passenger train. No 70032 was withdrawn in September 1967 from neighbouring Kingmoor and stored there for a further five months before being cut up at McWilliams, Shettleston in March 1968.   **21st MAY 1966 ● R.S. GREENWOOD**

CARLISLE (KINGMOOR)

Ivatt 'Mogul' 2-6-0's were rare birds in the Manchester area, apart from those regularly observed on Bolton shed, ex-Horwich Works, which was responsible for the overhaul of members of the class. No **43023** from Carlisle Kingmoor may possibly be on its way there or, if not, had been borrowed, as Kingmoor had no booked workings to Agecroft at the time.

8th JANUARY 1961 ● KEN NUTTALL

50 A

YORK

Ex-LNER B1 No 61038 *Blacktail* is stabled in the shed yard for the afternoon. This was a daily occurrence (SX) with the locomotive arriving at Manchester Victoria at 12.07pm (ex-10.10am York), It deposited the empty stock at Irlam Carriage Sidings before coming on shed for servicing. It returned home on the 5.10pm from Victoria. *Blacktail* didn't stay long at York, moving on to Leeds Neville Hill in May 1957. **1956 ● C.A. APPLETON**

19 B

SHEFFIELD (MILLHOUSES)

L&Y engines out-stationed at Hull (No 12) and York (No 13) were under the supervision of Agecroft prior to the Grouping. The Midland vacated their roundhouse at the south end of York station about 1928 and joined the former L&Y at Queen Street shed. In 1932 they moved once more to the former Great North of England straight shed but lost their own allocation here prior to the war. Express workings to Liverpool Exchange and Manchester Victoria were ex-Midland turns and Sheffield Millhouses provided the motive power before the ex-LNER Clifton shed took over in BR days. Inside Cylinder 2P 4-4-0 No **602** stands under the coal stage after working in with the morning York train. By Nationalisation this engine had disappeared north to Kingmoor. **c.1938 ● A.G. ELLIS**

Jubilee 4-6-0 No 45564 *New South Wales* stands in the yard with a 'Not to be Moved' disc clipped on to the window, immediately above the cabside number. This suggests that the loco failed en-route in the area as Holbeck certainly had no workings to Agecroft. Such a discovery would have delighted the local enthusiasts as it was rare to find a visiting named engine here. Two 'Crab' 2-6-0s occupy the same road, the nearest of which is No **42901** (26B).

9th JUNE 1963 ● GORDON COLTAS

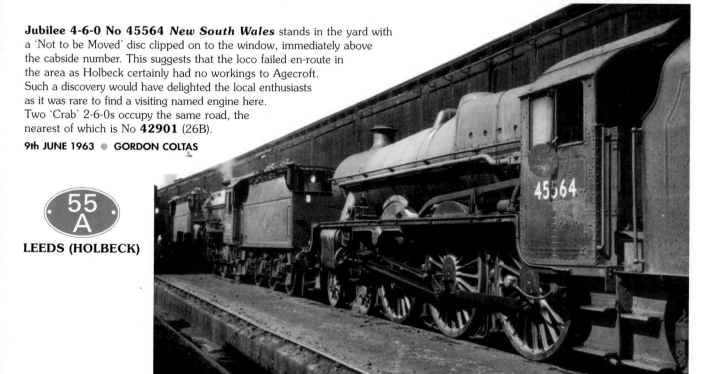

55 A

LEEDS (HOLBECK)

One of Agecroft's last Class Fives, No 45096 stands on No 2 road inside the shed with its cab is shrouded in steam during a routine boiler washout. A BR diesel-electric shunter is also evident, tucked away in the corner on No 1 road. **SEPTEMBER 1966** ● **TONY RENSHAW**

The Prototype Standard Class Five No 73000 was an unexpected arrival in April 1966. The loco first emerged from Derby Works in April 1951 when it would seem that the authorities placed the locomotive on trial. By the end of the year it had appeared at Perth, Derby and Stratford! It settled on the ex-Midland lines in the 1950's, running out of Nottingham and Grimesthorpe, although by September 1962 was at Woodford Halse on the ex-GC. When that shed became 1G (formerly 2F) in September 1963, many of its locos had the plates removed and a stencilled 1G within a white oval line applied instead. In January 1965 Oxley received the loco and three months later it was off again to Shrewsbury. These two sheds presumably re-attached backing and shedplates to No 73000. Before it arrived at Agecroft, Shrewsbury had removed its plates to reveal the old code but left the securing bolts. The last move in October 1966, was to nearby Patricroft where a 9H plate was affixed until withdrawal in March 1968.

SEPTEMBER 1966 ● **TONY RENSHAW**

The new single pitched roof covering four roads had recently been completed when this interior view was taken. The shed roof, and in particular, the smoke vents, would be subjected to another 30 years of sulphurous emissions and the comparison with the photograph above is interesting. In many respects Agecroft was little different from other sheds but the added disadvantage was that the land on which the shed stood was always vulnerable to subsidence. It was rumoured that closure was accelerated when large cracks suddenly appeared in the Shedmaster's office wall. Ex-L&Y 2F 0-6-0ST No **11421** stands within the recesses of the shed building, out of steam, but would eventually receive the fireraiser's attention when it was next delegated for duty on the Engine Arrangements Board.

SEPTEMBER 1938 ● **GORDON COLTAS**

A grubby Stanier 8F, No 48224, drifts on to the shed only days before its closure. By this time Agecroft's allocation consisted of 19 members of this class supported by 8 Stanier Class Fives and 5 of the Standard variety. The only other engine was 'Jinty' 0-6-0 No 47202, which was later stored at the side of Patricroft 'old' shed awaiting a decision on its future. Note the sprinkler gear with counter balance near the ash pits which helped keep dust down, making life slightly more tolerable for the disposal men.   **SEPTEMBER 1966 ● TONY RENSHAW**

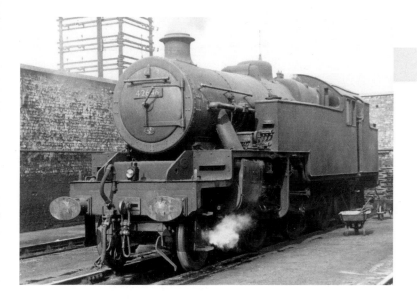

BR DAYS

During the LMS period, Agecroft's original shed roof was removed and, because of subsidence problems, only four of the eight roads were re-covered in the new single pitch style favoured by the Company. A wooden wall partitioned the two sections and the southerly half of the shed was left exposed to the elements. Stanier Class 4 2-6-4T No **42646** stands at the back of the open roads awaiting its next duty. By the early 1960's, the shed had little suitable work for engines of this kind and their last two, Nos 42474 and 42647 left for pastures new in October 1963.

1961 ● J. DAVENPORT

The servicing facilities at Agecroft were much improved after 1937 when the installation of automatic coal & ash handling apparatus was completed. The coaling plant consisted of two 75 ton bunkers and an electrically driven hoist. In common with many other ex-L&Y depots, the original 'coal hole' with water tank over survived as a water tank only. Ex-L&Y Class 'A' 0-6-0 No **52461** stands alongside one of the water columns which also once belonged to that Company. In 1945 the shed had 14 members of the 'A' class but lost their last when No 52293 moved to Lees (Oldham) in April 1955. Irlam Carriage Shed building, which accommodated up to 60 coaches, is visible, standing between the Fast and Slow lines between Pendleton and Pendlebury.

c.1948 ● PAUL SHACKCLOTH COLLECTION

A fine panoramic view of the yard was available from the lofty heights of the coaling stage. One assumes that photographer Alex Appleton had permission to clamber up the ladder to obtain this shot. B1 4-6-0 No **61038** *Blacktail* and a Stanier Class 4 2-6-4T occupy the shed yard behind which is the foreman's office complete with bay window. Jinty 0-6-0 No **47579** shares one of the outer roads with the Departmental Van and a rather clean Ivatt Class 2 2-6-0 No **46486**. Sister engines No 46412 and No 46485 arrived in November 1953 for shunting duties at Oldfield Road and Hope Street to replace the ageing ex-L&Y 0-6-0 Saddle Tanks. They were joined three months later by No 46486.   1956 ● C.A. APPLETON

Chalked around the cab side number are the words *Boiler Empty - Joe Knowles*. Agecroft 'Pug' 0-4-0ST No **51207** has probably been serviced and received a boiler washout on its weekend sojourn back at the shed and the message may well be for the attention of the steam raiser. The shunting engine is sandwiched between the Departmental Van and WD 2-8-0 No **90102**, whose number is conveniently legible through the porthole at the rear of the cab. The Austerity arrived off the Western Region in November 1950 going later to Wigan and then on to nearby Bolton where it stayed until withdrawal in November 1963.

c.1960 ● J. DAVENPORT

A class of locos that were associated with many of the ex-L&Y engine sheds were the 'Crabs'. After their introduction in 1926, Agecroft always had a sizeable allocation to call on and in 1945 they had 21 on the books - more than any other 'Lanky' shed. They were regularly used on the Normanton passenger services over the Calder Valley main line for many years as well as a multitude of other duties. No **2734** was a long standing resident which eventually moved away to Wigan in BR days in February 1960. Together with No 42755, the engine took a four month sabbatical between January and April 1953 over the border at Dalry Road (64C)!

17th AUGUST 1947 ● K. FAIREY

Fowler 7F 0-8-0 No 49668 stands over the pits, ready for duty, in the exposed part of the shed. These rugged looking locos, designed by Sir Henry Fowler, were introduced in April 1929. The last six survivors of a class originally numbering 175 engines ended up at Agecroft and on 1st January 1961 were amongst the shed's allocation of 51 locos which comprised the following:

Class 4 2-6-4T: 42474, 42646/7
Class 6P5F 2-6-0: 42723/4/5/53/5, 42819/60/8
Class 5 4-6-0: 44781/2, 44823, 44929/87, 45261, 45337/8
Class 2 2-6-0: 46485/6
Class 3F 0-6-0T: 47224, 47574/8/9
Class 7F 0-6-0: 49505/8, 49618/27/37/68
Class 0F 0-4-0ST: 51204/7/29
Class 2F 0-6-0ST: 51413/96
Class B1 4-6-0: 61008 *Kudu*, 61201/69/98, 61369
WD Class 8F 2-8-0: 90292, 90307/24/54/59/72, 90546/58, 90626/32

No 49668 was withdrawn in November 1961 and No 49508, the last of the class, two months later.

30th SEPTEMBER 1961 ● N. MACHELL

'Jinty' 0-6-0 No 47202 drifts down the shed yard. The Johnson veteran, dating from 1899, was fitted with condensing apparatus for working on the Metropolitan Widened Lines. The pipes and operational gear rod remained in-situ after the loco came north. After a spell at Fleetwood and Horwich Works shunter, it came to Agecroft before moving on to Newton Heath.

JUNE 1966 ● SALFORD LOCAL HISTORY LIBRARY

WD 2-8-0 No 90142 stands in light steam outside the foreman's office. The loco was constructed at the Hyde Park Works of North British in 1943 and great numbers of the class eventually gravitated on to the Central Division after having been officially purchased by British Railways in October 1948. Prior to this, the loco was one of 50 which the Southern Region had on loan in the intermediate period. It ran from Feltham and Hither Green sheds in the London area before coming north in June 1951. No 90142 arrived at Agecroft from Newton Heath in May 1961.

NOVEMBER 1961 ● IAN COCKCROFT

B1 4-6-0 No 61008 *Kudu* stands in the shed yard. This was the first 'named' locomotive to come on to the allocation.

18th OCTOBER 1959 ● H.K. BOULTER

It came as a surprise when five ex-LNER B1 4-6-0's arrived at the ex-L&Y shed from Leicester (GC) between August and October 1959. They were Nos 61008 *Kudu*, 61201/69/98 and 61369. The intention was to use the engines on Agecroft's remaining principal turns over the Calder Valley route from Manchester Victoria to Normanton and York, but in the event, they did little passenger work. They were unpopular with the 'Lanky' men who always preferred the 'Crabs' and Class Fives. No 61369 was the last to arrive and was immediately dispatched to Darlington Works for overhaul. This was followed by No 61201, which was involved in a minor collision at Ancoats Goods Depot and was then repaired locally at the parent depot, Newton Heath. This may well have been the first, and only time that an ex-LNER engine entered the 'Parlour'. It became one of the first casualties of the 410 strong class, being withdrawn in January 1962. Three months later, *Kudu* left for Woodford Halse whilst Nos 61269 and 61369 moved on locally to the ex-Great Central shed at Gorton where, no doubt, they were found to be more popular, especially as they were the last two ex-LNER engines left there. Two months later, No 61298 was withdrawn from service, thus ending Agecroft's association with the B1 class.

B1 4-6-0 No 61369 in the yard, showing signs of smokebox scorching.

8th JANUARY 1961 ● KEN NUTTALL

JUBILEES

In common with other sheds whose duties were mainly freight, Agecroft had a brief flirtation with a number of Jubilees displaced from main line duties. They arrived in two batches of four. Nos 45590 *Travancore*, 45607 *Fiji*, 45654 *Hood* and 45664 *Nelson* came from Sheffield Millhouses in February/March 1962 and four months later, Nos 45716 *Swiftsure*, 45718 *Dreadnought*, 45728 *Defiance* and 45729 *Furious* arrived from Carlisle Kingmoor. The last three were withdrawn after barely three months service, as was *Fiji* during November 1962. The remaining four were transferred away to 26A in June 1963.

By October 1962, Agecroft was no longer using any of its four ex-Sheffield Jubilees and these, together with *Swiftsure,* were stored serviceable in the open. No **45654 *Hood*** moved on to Newton Heath with *Swiftsure* in June 1963 and, after a spell away at Stockport Edgeley between March 1964 and October 1965, returned to become Newton Heath's last Jubilee and was withdrawn in June 1966. *Hood* was in a presentable condition and very much in service when recorded standing at the side of Agecroft shed between duties. **17th JUNE 1962 ● PAUL SHACKCLOTH COLLECTION**

No 45716 *Swiftsure* is in store at the end of the line in the roofless part of the shed, still displaying its nameplates and front number. This Jubilee remained coupled to a Fowler 3,500 gallon tender until withdrawal, which was unusual for the class. **NOVEMBER 1962 ● IAN COCKCROFT**

The climb from Pendleton to Pendlebury at 1 in 72/99 was followed followed by sharp undulations and slacks over many colliery workings. This low angle view shows off the majestic lines of the rebuilt Royal Scot 4-6-0 class to great advantage. In September 1961, Newton Heath took delivery of four members, Nos 46133 *The Green Howards*, 46139 *The Welch Regiment*, 46140 *The King's Royal Rifle Corps* and 46142 *The York & Lancaster Regiment*, all of which had been displaced at Kentish Town by 'Peak" main line diesels operating on the Midland main line. No **46140 *The King's Royal Rifle Corps*** nears the top of Pendlebury bank with the 6.10pm SX Manchester Victoria to Southport express.   **26th APRIL 1963 ● E.F. BENTLEY**

IRLAMS O' TH' HEIGHT STATION

An unidentified ex-L&Y 4-4-2 'Highflyer' calls at Irlams O' Th' Height station with a Manchester bound stopping train. The entrance was between the underbridge on Green Lane via a flight of steps directly on to the island platform. The station opened in 1901 serving the Slow Lines only and was convenient for Agecroft Shed and the neighbouring colliery and dye works.   **c.1904** ● **PAUL SHACKCLOTH COLLECTION**

Looking east towards Manchester. The original L&Y building and platform are of timber construction with only the chimneys in brick. This low level view is of much interest and features two members of staff posing behind a platform seat turned to face the camera for what must obviously be an official photograph. It was taken 11 years after the station's opening, probably to either record the upgrading of certain facilities here or for publicity purposes. Under the canopy and behind the station nameboard is what appears to be a portable stepladder. Within the frame of this stepladder is a bank of five signal levers on the platform itself which can only have controlled the Up and Down Home Starter Signals. In 1917 - during the Great War and a period of acute manpower shortage, the L&Y appointed its first Station Mistress to work here.

1912 ● **J. ALSOP**

Despite the station's relative isolation and as a consequence, limited patronage, the LMS invested in the facilities here. The wooden trusses supporting the original timber platform have been replaced by a standard pre-cast pattern over which now stand conventional platform edging stones. The glazed canopy has made way for one of more austere design as have the gas lamps. The station nameboard has disappeared completely along with the signal levers and the station was to close completely on 5th March 1956. The lone figure on the platform is none other than Richard Casserley, son of the eminent photographer, Henry Casserley.

23rd APRIL 1951 ● **H.C. CASSERLEY**

PENDLEBURY BANK - THE SLOW LINES

Toiling up the Slow Line and about to pass through Irlams O' Th' Height Station is Fowler 0-8-0 No **49637** (27D - Wigan) with a train of coal. The headshunt and rear of the Irlam Carriage Shed building are both visible at a lower level. One of the veteran 0-4-4 tank engines from the Barton Wright era of the Lancashire & Yorkshire Railway could be found here for many years, acting as a stationary boiler to steam heat the coaching stock.

23rd APRIL 1951 ● H.C. CASSERLEY

One of Newton Heath's small but efficient Ivatt Class 2 2-6-0's, No 46437 is unusually employed on a stopping passenger to Wigan Wallgate. The loco frequently appeared on the Divisional Engineer's trains over the Central Division, which accounts for its cleanliness.

3rd OCTOBER 1957 ● W.D. COOPER

Many of the Blackpool 'residentials' travelled by way of the Liverpool line as far as Dobbs Brow Junction before taking the spur through Hilton House to join the Preston line at Horwich Fork Junction near Blackrod. This avoided passing through the busy environs of Bolton and the 'Blackpool Club Train' followed this route, departure from Manchester Victoria in later years being at 5.16pm. It went non-stop to Lytham and with further calls at Ansdell, St. Annes, Squires Gate and Blackpool South, the train was due to arrive at Blackpool Central at 6.46pm. The morning journey departed at 7.40pm, arriving in Manchester at 9.15am and in addition to the above named stations, picked up at Kirkham and Chorley before calling at Salford for those who had business in that part of the city. A regular performer was a long standing resident - Blackpool Jubilee 4-6-0 No **45705** *Seahorse,* seen here storming up the bank with an express bound for its home town.

28th AUGUST 1961 ● W.D. COOPER

L&Y converted 0-6-0 Saddletank No 532 is in a spot of bother near Pendlebury. Both the Newton Heath and Sandhills Breakdown Trains are in attendance and the cranes are working in joint operation. The larger of the two, No 2188, a 35 ton steam crane built by Craven Brothers in March 1911 and belonging to Sandhills, is at the rear. Prominent in the foreground dealing with the smokebox end of the loco is No 2231, Newton Heath's steam crane which was a Cowans, Sheldon product of 1906 and capable of lifting 25 tons. The L&Y were well catered for in this respect with a 30 ton steam crane being stationed at Wakefield. Eleven other sheds on the system had 10/20 ton hand cranes, whilst in addition, a further five sheds had tool vans but no crane.

1912 ● ALLAN SOMMERFIELD COLLECTION

PENDLEBURY BANK - THE FAST LINES

With safety valves blowing off, Stanier Class Five No **45076** nears the top of the bank on the approach to Pendlebury Station with a Southport express. The splitting signal for the Down Slow indicates the facility for trains to transfer on to the Down Fast.

MAY 1958 ● W.D. COOPER

An Agecroft Jubilee at work. A summer Saturday excursion train composed of non-corridor stock is in the hands of a rather decrepit member, No **45607** *Fiji,* which has reached the top of the bank and is showing inter-regional Reporting Number 1X87. The crossover connecting the Up and Down Fast with the Slow Lines which pass through Irlams o' th' Height Station is in the foreground.

**4th AUGUST 1962 ●
D. HAMPSON**

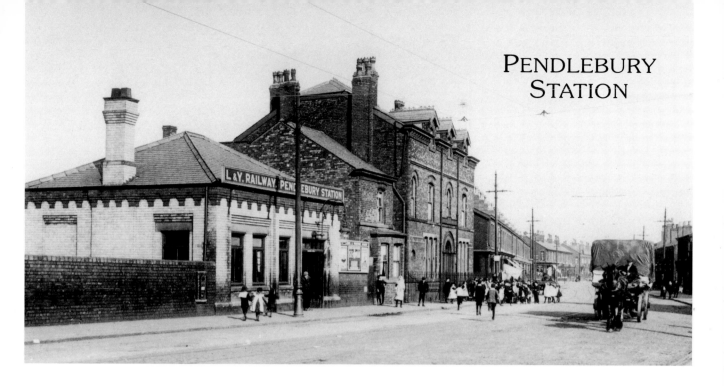

The building at Pendlebury Station, situated between Pendleton and Swinton, was rich in architectural detail. The L&Y, seeking conformity, built the next two stations on the Hindley line - those at Swinton and Moorside and Wardley, in similar style. This view is looking down Bolton Road in the Irlams o' th' Height direction and whilst a horse and cart comes trundling by in time honoured fashion, the driver is seemingly oblivious to the small boys running across the road towards a mystery activity, which has already attracted the attention of a large number of children. **1897 ● ALLAN SOMMERFIELD COLLECTION**

A Southport Stanier Class 4 2-6-4T No 42435 bursts out of the short Pendlebury tunnel, showing express head-lamps, on the Down Fast line. A number of tightly timed trains between Manchester and the Lancashire coastal town, calling at Wigan Wallgate only, were in the hands of these trusty engines. **1962 ● W.D. COOPER**

By May 1960, Britannia Pacific No 70045 *Lord Rowallan* had already been relegated to secondary duties by the authorities at Newton Heath, having arrived there only five months earlier, together with No 70048 *The Territorial Army 1908-58*. Their transfer to the Central Lines depot was specifically to work the accelerated timetable between Manchester Victoria and Glasgow Central. The Newton Heath enginemen, fiercely proud of their Jubilees, won the day, and *Tobago* etc. soon resumed normal service. *Lord Rowallan* disappeared to Neasden in September 1961. The Pacific is again working a Southport train at the same location.

24th MAY 1960 ● W.D. COOPER

SWINTON LUT GARAGE

No 420, a Dennis Lance 6LW of 1949 stands resplendent outside Swinton Garage. It was opened in 1906 to serve the newly constructed South Lancashire Tramways Company routes through Boothstown, Worsley, Swinton and Walkden. The location was at the south end of Partington Lane where provision was made for seven tram roads with an extension to accommodate buses being added at a later date.

c.1960 ● DAVID YOUNG COLLECTION

SOUTH LANCASHIRE TRANSPORT CO LTD

SLT operated an extensive system of inter-urban routes covering over 30 route miles, extending from Farnworth in the east to St. Helens in the west. Plans to develop the network into the heart of Salford never materialised, although a route reached Bolton whose Corporation-owned trolley-buses worked the service. These were operated by SLT. The fleet of 71 vehicles contained many interesting examples, several of which were introduced in 1930 and lasted throughout the Company's 28 year existence. No **20**, a Guy BTX of Wolverhampton with lowbridge Roe bodywork & Metrovick electrical equipment dates from 1931, but was later re-styled during the early 1950's to give a more modern appearance. It stands outside Swinton Hospital and is turning from Vicarage Road on to Partington Lane, which offered a connection with the rather curious 14 mile route from Atherton to Farnworth - by way of Worsley, Swinton, Walkden and Little Hulton. The last day of operation was 31st August 1958, after which SLT was absorbed by the Lancashire United Transport Company. **c.1957 ● J. FOZARD**

SWINTON HOSPITAL

JOINT SERVICES

The crew of Manchester Corporation No 3330 take a well earned breather at the terminus. Their bus, a Leyland PD2/12 with Leyland body and new in July 1953, was the first member of a batch of 40, all of which were based at Hyde Road Garage. No 3330 is standing at Swinton Church on Service 57 before departing for Thornley Park - on the boundary between Gorton and Denton. This service, along with Service 77 (on which No **3334** can also be seen working), was introduced in 1951 and was jointly operated with Salford City Transport, whose buses ran out of Weaste Garage. No 3368 in the series survives in private preservation.

21st JUNE 1955 ● E. GRAY

SWINTON STATION

Swinton Station, in common with neighbours Pendlebury and Moorside & Wardley, served the Slow lines only. All three had architectural similarities, offering passenger access at street level, descending to the island platforms by staircase. The building is situated within the overbridge carrying the aptly named Station Road, which ran from the town centre north to Bolton Road. The name Station Road was familiar in Rugby League circles too - as the home of Swinton Rugby League Club, whose main stand can be seen behind the upper quadrant signal. This ground, whose capacity was 44,000, staged many important games over the years including International matches against Australia and New Zealand. It also acted as a neutral venue for Challenge Cup semi-finals, no doubt influenced by the close proximity of the station. Swinton 'Lions' halcyon years were in the early 1960's under the captaincy of Albert Blan, when they were league champions in successive seasons. International players Ken Gowers, Alan Buckley and John Stopford were members of a threequarter line generally acknowledged to be one of the finest that ever graced the game. The Club's fortunes ultimately suffered and although the ground outlived the age of steam, it was sold for housing development and no trace of the ground now remains. **c.1968 ● ALLAN SOMMERFIELD**

MOORSIDE AND WARDLEY

Ex-Midland locos were a rare sight on this stretch of line. Deeley 3F 0-6-0 No **3630,** a veteran of 1903, rattles its train towards Walkden near Moorside & Wardley Station. The loco was a Belle Vue member until that shed closed in April 1956, at which time it moved 'over the line' to Gorton until withdrawal in September 1959.

17th MARCH 1947 ● W.D. COOPER

Stanier Class Five 4-6-0 No 44736 hurries the 6.10pm Manchester Victoria to Southport express through Moorside and Wardley. This train, which departed from Platform 12, picked up at Pendleton Broad Street before stopping at Wigan Wallgate and Meols Cop only. An all stations train (except Meols Cop) to Southport, which had left Platform 14 five minutes earlier, was usually overtaken by the express in this vicinity. The coaches are one of three ex-Coronation Scot articulated sets which were regularly used on the service. The engine returned home with the 9.00pm via Bolton.

6th JULY 1956 ● B.K.B. GREEN

The Lancashire and Yorkshire Railway provided ten sets of water troughs at various locations over their system. Those at Smithy Bridge, Sowerby Bridge, Horbury Junction, Kirkby, Whitley Bridge and Lostock Junction were heated during frosty weather whilst those at Lea Road, Hoscar, Rufford & Walkden Troughs, situated between Moorside & Wardley and Walkden stations were not. A Stanier Class 4 2-6-4T No **42656** from Bolton (26C) is handling an express passenger working and is passing over the troughs on its way to Manchester. The Fowler tender on the adjacent Down Slow line possibly belongs to a 'Crab' 2-6-0.

2nd SEPTEMBER 1962 ● W.D. COOPER

WALKDEN TROUGHS

Britannia Pacific No 70034, formerly *Thomas Hardy*, makes its way towards Wigan on the slow line with a stopping train. Newton Heath took delivery of this engine and three other 'Brits' from Crewe South in July 1965, Nos 70017 *Arrow*, 70021 *Morning Star* and 70044 *Earl Haig*. All four were in pretty poor condition when they arrived and all moved away after May 1966. *Earl Haig* went to Stockport Edgeley whilst the others went north to what was commonly referred to as the Britannia shed - Carlisle Kingmoor.

FEBRUARY 1966 ● W.D. COOPER

Jubilee 4-6-0 No 45584 *North West Frontier* replenishes its tender and more on the way home to Blackpool with one of the many residential expresses. Local photographer Wilf Cooper, who obviously had a lineside permit, must have been prepared to receive a soaking in order to obtain this spectacular photograph.

17th MARCH 1961 ● W.D. COOPER

WALKDEN (HIGH LEVEL)

Long serving Blackpool Class Five 4-6-0 No 44737 blasts through Walkden (High Level) on the Up Fast with an express for Manchester. The exhaust from the engine is nicely back lit which has helped create this rather dramatic image. At least three passengers have ascended the covered stairway from the booking office, on to the island platform to await the next local train to Wigan.　**c.1961** ● **IAN COCKCROFT**

A Fairburn 2-6-4T No 42132 belonging to Southport shed, heads through Walkden at speed with an express bound for its home town. Many of the enginemen from the seaside depot took a great pride in the performance of their tank engines. Some considered it a matter of honour not to exceed 750 gallons of water on the more lightly loaded trains over the route, which covered nearly 36 miles.

c.1961 ● **IAN COCKCROFT**

A stopping train gets away from Walkden behind ex-L&Y Class 3P 'Radial' 2-4-2T No **10923**. This was the only example to be based at Wigan (L&Y) which had been rebuilt in 1914 with Belpaire boiler and Schmidt superheater. The other eight locos of the class allocated were in original condition and, as such, were classified 2P. It was unusual to find this loco still working the Manchester turns as by this date the shed had LMS Class 4 motive power in the shape of Fowler (3), Stanier (6) and Fairburn (2) tank examples. Note the ex-L&Y vintage coach behind the engine.

10th SEPTEMBER 1945 ● **W.D. COOPER**

PENDLETON (OLD) STATION

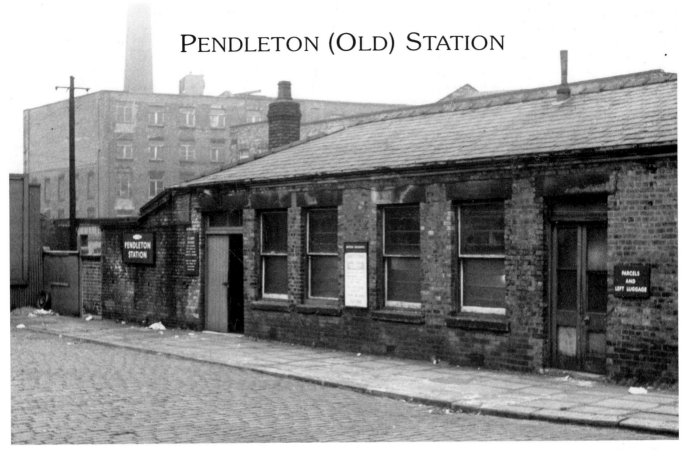

One suspects that if this photograph had been taken 100 years earlier, nothing except for the signage would have changed. Pendleton Station, to give it its proper name, first opened in August 1843 - five years after the formation of the *'Manchester and Bolton Railway'*. Although not appearing in the timetable as such, it was always referred to as Pendleton 'Old', certainly in recent years - perhaps to differentiate from neighbouring Pendleton Broad Street which opened much later on 1st June 1889 and was known as Pendleton 'New'. Indeed, the Station Announcers at Manchester Victoria called it Pendleton 'Old' until closure on 5th December 1966.   **1966 ● T. FLETCHER**

Standing on the towpath of the Manchester, Bury and Bolton Canal, photographer John Clarke has recorded Carlisle (Kingmoor) Britannia Pacific No **70021**, formerly ***Morning Star***, approaching Pendleton (Old) Station. This lay midway between Agecroft Junction and Windsor Bridge on the direct line from Manchester Victoria to Bolton Trinity Street. The lengthy train of empty parcels vans is destined for Red Bank Carriage Sidings. Agecroft coal hopper looms deceptively close in the background.   **27th SEPTEMBER 1967 ● JOHN CLARKE**

Taken from a passing train, Graham Whitehead has recorded the ex-L&Y signalbox named Brindle Heath Sidings Cabin, which controlled Brindle Heath Old Sidings (low level). They were also referred to as the 'Duchy' Sidings and were situated on the Down side of the line between Pendleton Old Station and Agecroft Junction beyond Holland Street bridge. On the Up side, the site was originally occupied by Pendleton Colliery which had been taken over by the Manchester Oxide Company in 1942. The LMS laid new sidings which remained in operation until 1963 by which time Manchester chemical firm Hardman and Holden were in control. To the right of the box, a WD 2-8-0 can be glimpsed on the connecting line between Brindle Heath Junction and Agecroft Junction whilst to the left is the Junction signalbox.

25th SEPTEMBER 1962 ●
GRAHAM WHITEHEAD

AGECROFT JUNCTION

An unidentified Stanier Class Five showing Class 'A' lamps brings a mixed bag of coaching stock towards Manchester from the Clifton Junction direction. The distinctive lines of a former Great Western Second coach is immediately behind the tender.

AUGUST 1953 ● TREVOR MOSELEY COLLECTION

Park House Bridge was an excellent vantage point to observe traffic passing through Agecroft Junction. Ex-LMS 0-8-0 No **49603** reverses a rake of empty mineral wagons into Agecroft Power Station off the Pendleton 'Old' line. Note the two new BR 16 ton examples which are mixed in with the older wooden variety. The Brake Van next to the engine suggests that this may well be a transfer to Ordsall Lane, in which case the engine will run around it's train in the Manchester Exchange area. The prominent guy ropes offer extra stability to the high Home Starter signal for the Connecting Line which made sighting possible east of Park House Bridge. A tank engine stands just beyond the signalbox and is probably waiting for a path to Agecroft Shed. The south bank of the *Manchester, Bolton and Bury Canal*, disused after 1936, is prominent whilst the cooling towers belonging to Agecroft Power Station dominate the horizon.

9th JUNE 1954 ● B.K.B. GREEN

CEGB AGECROFT

Salford's first power station opened at Wallness Road in August 1895 and was replaced six years later by another at Frederick Road which was situated between the railway and canal. In 1921, new facilities were developed at Agecroft (the 'A' station), on land east of the Manchester to Bolton line between Agecroft and Clifton Junctions. Frederick Road was then relegated to a sub-station. After World War Two, further facilities (the 'B' station) were developed on an adjacent site and both became the property of the British Electricity Authority after the Nationalisation of the industry in 1948. Expanding the facilities even more, a third power station (the 'C' station) opened in 1962. All three were still functioning at the end of the BR steam period but closed in 1970, 1980 & 1993 respectively, by which time the industry had been privatised. The cooling towers were demolished a year later.

Two four coupled saddle tanks built by Robert Stephenson and Hawthorns Ltd were delivered to work the new sidings as Agecroft 'B' station began operations in 1950. Both engines carried nameplates. *Agecroft No 1* and *Agecroft No 2* came in an attractive green livery, fully lined out in black, yellow and red. A third, identical engine arrived in 1954 and was named *Agecroft No 3*. The industry experienced further reorganisation and by 1958 it had become the Central Electricity Generating Board. **Agecroft No 2** hurries back to the shed but hiding behind the engine's exhaust and running parallel is Class 40 No **324** on the main line with a goods train. Under the grime, No 2 had been repainted in unlined blue whilst sister engines Nos 1 and 3 were finished in red and green.

4th FEBRUARY 1973 ● GORDON COLTAS

THE BELFAST BOAT EXPRESS

The last regular steam hauled named train on BR was the *Belfast Boat Express*. The daily service ran from Heysham to Manchester Victoria but as there was no boat on Sunday evenings or Monday mornings, it ran to and from Morecambe Promenade and carried no headboard on those occasions. After the war, Carnforth provided Stanier Class Fives but had Jubilees to call on in the early 1960's. Metrovick Co-Bo Diesel-Electrics took over in 1963 but they proved prone to failure. This opened the way for a unique and most welcome return to steam in 1965 and Stanier Class Fives were once more employed. A clean example, No **45025** passes Agecroft Junction on the direct line with the very last Up train, complete with a smart set of blue and grey coaches. The previous day, and to much acclaim, No 45342 left Victoria's No 12 platform with the last Down train. The engine carried an extra headboard commemorating the event. No 45025 survives in preservation and is based at the *Strathspey Railway,* north of the border. **5th MAY 1968 ● R.W. MILLER**

Subsidence caused by coal mining was a problem in the area. Agecroft Junction Signalbox, a L&Y structure dating back to 1902, began to develop a pronounced inward lean after the war and by 1950, the structure was rendered unsafe. The replacement box, built almost opposite on the Down side was a LMR architect's designed building which benefited from having a modern kitchen area, flush toilets and central heating. Signalling and Telegraph Department personnel are in the course of providing new mechanical connections and point rodding which would render the box operational later that year. The portable blacksmith's anvil and 'Holliday and Onions' forge were an essential part of the fitting out process of mechanical connections. An Accrington 'Crab' 2-6-0 No **42718** drifts by between the boxes, routed on the direct line via Pendleton (Old) with an Up stopping train.   **31st MAY 1950** ● **G. SHUTTLEWORTH**

Although coal was delivered directly to Agecroft Power Station by conveyor belt from the re-opened local colliery, a considerable amount arrived by rail with Bickershaw and certain Yorkshire collieries being the main providers. An unidentified BR 350hp six-coupled diesel electric locomotive is propelling a train of coal into the National Coal Board Sidings from the nearby Brindle Heath Old Sidings. Agecroft B & C Power Stations are in view behind the signalbox. The original splitting signal west of the junction on the Up side had been replaced some time after the new box had been brought into commission in 1950.

31st MAY 1964 ● **JOHN CLARKE**

The Reporting Number W426 carried by the Pilot engine, Stanier Class Five 4-6-0 No **44658** from Nottingham shed (16A), represented the Summer Saturdays Only 12.30pm Abergele to Manchester Victoria, which arrived in the city from the north east direction, having been routed from Warrington via Skelton Junction, Stockport Edgeley, Denton and Droylsden Junctions. This lengthy train may well have been extended to Bolton or a similar Lancashire town on this occasion. An unidentified Standard Caprotti Class Five is the train engine, which was an unusual sight over ex-L&Y metals in this area.

7th SEPTEMBER 1960 ● **W.D. COOPER**

CLIFTON JUNCTION

A L&Y Radial 2-4-2 tank is about to depart from Clifton Junction Station with a Manchester bound stopping train. The East Lancashire line to Radcliffe and Bury is to the right whilst the signal in the background is the Molyneux Junction Starter on the LNWR line which passed under the station, beneath the Bolton platforms, and continued through Clifton Hall Tunnel towards Patricroft Junction.

c.1923 ● JOHN RYAN COLLECTION

Clifton Junction has a rather interesting history. The fascinating story with regard to *The Battle of Clifton Junction* arose as a result of the rivalry between the East Lancashire and the Lancashire and Yorkshire Railways. The Manchester to Bolton line was opened in May 1838 by the L&YR, with the station here first appearing in the public timetable in 1847. The ELR, branching north towards Bury, opened a year earlier in 1846. The ELR trains from Bury to Manchester used the L&Y facility beyond Clifton Junction by arrangement, paying a toll dependent on the number of passengers carried, and as a result all trains stopped here. In a bid to attract more custom, the ELR wished to speed up their service by running non stop and they offered to submit their books to the L&Y Company for scrutinisation instead. The L&Y refused and the ELR insisted on running non stop. The result was a huge baulk of timber placed across the line by the L&Y, supported by a train of its own. The County Police were present in case of violence but the ELR retaliated by running a stone ballast train across the junction, thereby preventing the L&Y from running its own service to Bolton. In the meantime numerous other trains were 'jammed' in the area. Common sense eventually prevailed and a certain Mr. Blackhouse, on behalf of the L&Y, ordered that the lines be cleared. After negotiation, a *Treaty of Manchester* was signed and East Lancashire trains passed through without stopping after all.

The **'Rossendale Forester'** was a farewell railtour organised by the *North West Branch of the Locomotive Club of Great Britain.* The locomotives involved were Ivatt Class 2 2-6-0 No 46437 from Newton Heath and Stanier Class 4 2-6-4T No **42644** from Trafford Park. The tank engine appears to be in typical condition and with the lack of headboard, one could be forgiven for believing that this was a normal service train. A trio of 'gricers' leaning out of the windows of the first coach rather gives the game away. No 42644 is about to become the last steam engine to traverse the former East Lancs main line between Clifton Junction and Radcliffe North Junction. The line was completely closed two days later.

3rd DECEMBER 1966 ● R.S. GREENWOOD

This commanding view looking north east across the Irwell Valley is immediately west of Clifton Junction. A 'Crab' 2-6-0, No **42701** drifts down the bank from the Bolton direction with a parcels train. The viaduct spanning the valley carried the East Lancs Railway line and was constructed in 1845. There is evidence that the former Robin Hood Sidings at low level in the foreground have recently been lifted. A few scattered sleepers remain but a connection once existed here, passing under the main line to connect with the former LNW branch which served the *Pilkington Tile and Pottery Works,* part of which stands behind the engine.   **c.1961 ● IAN COCKCROFT**

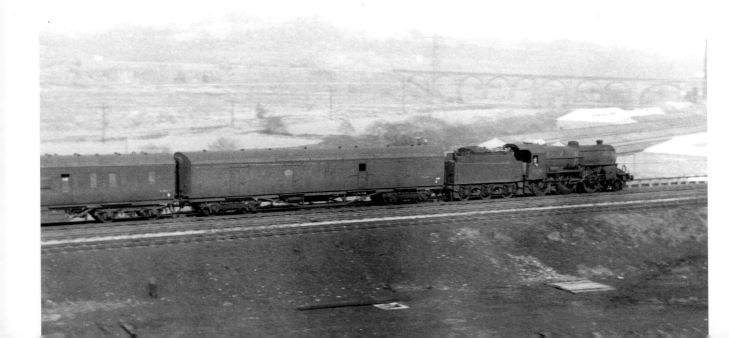

Approaching Kearsley is Stanier Class Five 4-6-0 No 44893 with the 11.15am Summer Saturdays Only Manchester Victoria to Blackpool North express. A number of mineral wagons occupy Kearsley Branch Sidings whilst beyond on the Up side stands Kearsley Junction Signalbox. The short branch from here to Linnyshaw Moss offered a connection with a system of colliery lines based at Walkden. The cooling towers and chimneys of Kearsley Power Station dominate the scene here. The site, which is on low ground beside the River Irwell, was formerly occupied by the Kearsley Hall Colliery. Electricity production commenced in 1929 with much of the coal coming from the nearby former Bridgewater pits. An electrified railway system existed within the complex and offered a connection with the former LMS branch sidings after passing under the main line on a severe gradient. A fleet of four locomotives were constantly employed transferring mineral wagons. By 1969 the power station, now operated by the Central Electricity Generating Board, was being run down but the rail system was further utilised for research purposes, attracting a variety of vehicles. Blackpool Twin Cars 689 and 690 were sold after withdrawal from service to GEC Traction who used them as a test bed for driverless control equipment. Both were then acquired by the ill- fated West Yorkshire Transport Museum in Bradford which when ultimately closed, the twin cars were disposed of. Kearsley also closed completely in 1985 at which time the cooling towers and chimneys were demolished.   **25th JUNE 1966** ● **E.F. BENTLEY**

MOLYNEUX BROW

The 4.20pm SX Manchester Victoria to Colne is approaching Molyneux Brow on the former East Lancs line. The train was booked to call at Salford, from where it had previously originated, and then run non stop to Accrington, followed by all stations to Colne. The Stanier 2-6-4 tank is No **42698** from Newton Heath, but the train always used to be one of Agecroft's premier duties.

11th MAY 1962 ● **C.A. APPLETON**

HEATON PARK

Heaton Park Station looking in the Prestwich direction on the Bury electrified line. A standard five car set of L&Y origin gets away from Platform 2, incorrectly displaying 'Manchester' within the destination panel. Heaton Park tunnel lies directly behind the photographer and it was here, during the Second World War, that drivers were known to have sheltered their trains for a period after air raid sirens had sounded. An Agecroft 'Crab' No **42725** passes in the Manchester direction, but, other than the afternoon pick-up goods train, steam locomotives traversing the line were sparse, although electrical engineering work on a Sunday occasionally resulted in a return to steam. During the winter of 1945, traffic was diverted this way as a result of a landslip in the Farnworth area on the Manchester to Bolton line. The evening train from Glasgow to Manchester Victoria was observed running late, passing through Crumpsall behind Polmadie Jubilee No 5584 *North West Frontier*. It would have travelled from Bolton Trinity Street by way of the junctions at Bradley Fold and Radcliffe West and East. Note the weighing machine on the Up platform - a common sight on many stations in the days of BR. **1950 ● STATIONS UK**

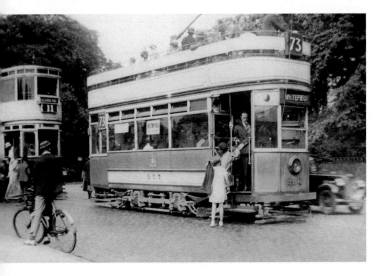

On hot summer's days, Heaton Park was a magnet for families from far and wide. The boating lake and bandstand were popular but many a small child would be content with a chance to sit on the lion statues guarding the entrance to the Hall. Hordes of passengers arrived by train, alighting at Heaton Park Station itself, or by tram. People wait patiently to alight, whilst children carefully step off the platform of Salford Car **296**, which had been re-numbered from No 66 in 1928. It was built in 1902 by G.F. Milnes and had Westinghouse electrical equipment and Brill trucks. As an open-top car, it was fitted with a vestibule during the early 1920's and was withdrawn in January 1937. The 73 route to Whitefield passed under the low bridge at Besses' O'Th' Barn and so until the arrival of the low-built and cut-down-height cars it was the province of open-toppers. Salford retained a few of these to work on summer days specifically to Heaton Park. Behind is a Manchester car on Service 11 - Alexandra Park to Heaton Park which became bus-operated in June 1937. The teenage cyclist caught observing the proceedings nicely completes the picture. **c.1935 ● M.J. O'CONNOR**

THOMAS WRIGLEY

Thomas Wrigley was a relatively small railway contracting family business based in Prestwich. The first known contract undertaken by the firm dates from April 1881 and it continued in business until acquired by Leonard Fairclough Ltd in 1951. A fleet of about 15 locomotives were in operation before the First World War but they were gradually withdrawn from service and by June 1943, *Princess* remained the sole survivor. This locomotive was a typical Manning Wardle Class E 0-4-0ST, Works No **1369**, constructed in 1897 and owned by Wrigley's since 1901. Its final job involved improvements to Irwell Park Wharf for the Manchester Ship Canal Company in 1951-1952, after which it returned to the firm's base at Prestwich Goods Yard where it was broken up in August 1953. *Princess* is pictured standing in the yard between contracts four years earlier. **2nd APRIL 1949 ● C.A. APPLETON**

BESSES O TH' BARN

Approaching the island platform at Besses o th' Barn Station from the Bury direction is the afternoon pick up goods. In the latter days the working was the province of one of Bury shed's Austerity 2-8-0 locos. No **90205** is about to cross Thatch Leach Lane bridge before trundling through the platform. Note the warning sign to 'keep off electric live rails'.   **10th OCTOBER 1963** ● **C.A. APPLETON**

WHITEFIELD

During the early tramcar days, those from Bury met their Salford counterparts at a point directly opposite Whitefield Station on Bury New Road, and each terminated there. As a consequence, passengers had the inconvenience of having to transfer from one car to another to continue their onward journey. In 1926, joint services were instigated but much traffic had already been lost to the newly electrified Manchester to Bury line. In later years, bus Service 17 ran from here to Victoria Bus Station and Daimler No **513** is performing that duty in March 1954. The following year, however, saw No 17 absorbed in Service 95, a newly created cross-city route extended to run between Whitefield and East Didsbury, via Broughton Bridge. It became one of the jointly operated services with Manchester City Transport.

MARCH 1954 ● **N.R. KNIGHT**

The following day, the same train is pictured passing through Whitefield and was in the hands of No **90364.** The sidings here stand empty and no longer would the engine set back. There were five Austerities left at Bury: Nos 90205, 90226, 90364, 90408 and 90419 and this particular example was fitted with a miniature snow plough.   **11th OCTOBER 1963** ● **C.A. APPLETON**

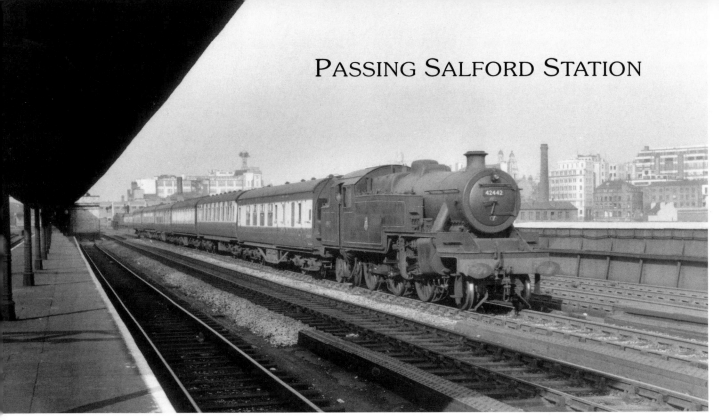

Platform 5 was an excellent vantage point to watch the trains go by, as all traffic leaving and entering Exchange station by-passed Salford Station on the south side. Stanier Class 4 2-6-4T No **42442** from Patricroft picks up speed on the Down Slow whilst working an all stations via Tyldesley to Liverpool Lime Street local passenger. In the distance is an unidentified Standard Class Five disappearing towards the city.   **c.1957 ● K. FIELD**

The 4.30pm Exchange to Llandudno which operated as the 'Club Train' on week-days, was often strengthened on Summer Saturdays. On this occasion a pair of grubby Stanier Class Fives, No **45316** piloting No **44780** are in charge of the train. The condition of these engines would not have been tolerated during the week. The pilot engine is carrying the correct Reporting Number for the train - 1D64.

24th AUGUST 1963 ● B.W.L. BROOKSBANK

One of Newton Heath's 'Crabs', No 42728 appears to have a train of non-corridor empty coaching stock from Ordsall Lane Carriage Sidings, yet is showing express lamps! The train is heading towards Exchange, or possibly Victoria Station on the Up Slow line.

c.1957 ● K. FIELD

Farnley Junction Jubilee 4-6-0 No 45646 *Napier* is seen carrying the St. Rollox style larger cab side numerals, having been transferred from Corkerhill in August 1952. It is being used on a filling-in turn, working a lightweight stopping passenger train from Manchester Exchange to Liverpool Lime Street.
17th OCTOBER 1953 ● TOM LEWIS

Approaching Manchester with an excursion train is Standard Class Five 4-6-0 No **73094.** Liverpool Road Goods Depot can be seen away to the left whilst the gantry carrying colour light signals on the curving viaduct for Down traffic acts as a frame for a 30cwt steam operated travelling crane. This was situated at low level within the Irwell Street Goods Yard complex. The Up and Down slow lines in the foreground were last used on 5th February 1968 and removed later that year. **c.1956 ● K. FIELD**

STANLEY STREET

A motley collection of road vehicles, some parked, some abandoned, are gathered at the far end of Stanley Street. Over the wall to the right was the original site of the 'old cloth shed' which was situated within the now abandoned Preston Yard. Behind the 'car park' sign once stood a 'checker's office' at the foot of the Oldfield Road incline. The personnel working from there recorded all wagon movements in and out of the yard. Crossing the bridge on the ex-LNWR line is an unidentified 8F 2-8-0 working tender first towards Ordsall Lane with a mixed freight.

JANUARY 1968 ● TONY RENSHAW

ORDSALL LANE

Approaching Ordsall Lane off the Castlefield Junction line is Standard Class 9F 2-10-0 No **92132** (8B-Warrington Dallam) with a train from Peak Forest to Duncan Street Exchange Sidings.

9th SEPTEMBER 1966 ● J.M. BENTLEY

Swinging off the viaduct and clattering over Ordsall Lane Junction is Stanier Class Five No **45033** (5B - Crewe South). The express passenger is on the Down Fast under clear signals whilst the Home and Distants on the Down Slow are also off. Local passenger services which previously used the line had been withdrawn and the likelihood is either a freight working, a light engine en-route to Patricroft shed or empty stock bound for nearby Ordsall Lane Carriage Sidings.

9th SEPTEMBER 1966 ● J.M. BENTLEY

A servicing facility remained in regular use at Ordsall Lane Junction until the end of steam in the Manchester area. A visiting Standard Class 9F 2-10-0 No **92249** from Speke Junction is taking water, having already made use of the 70ft turntable in readiness for its return to Liverpool. Blowing off steam in the background is one of Patricroft's Standard Caprotti Class Five 4-6-0's, No **73125**. Also within close proximity were Stanier 8F 2-8-0 No 48678 and English Electric six-coupled diesel shunter No D3592. Ordsall Lane No 1 signalbox controlled these and other movements in the vicinity of Liverpool Road Goods Station, access to which was gained from the Castlefield Junction line which is visible passing behind the signalbox.

6th MARCH 1968 ● TONY RENSHAW

LIVERPOOL ROAD STATION

On a fine Spring morning, ex-L&Y 'A' Class 0-6-0 No **52438** (8C - Speke Junction) is caught reversing five vestibuled coaches out of the original platform at Liverpool Road Station. The occasion was an 'Old Manchester Tour' organised jointly by the Manchester and Stephenson Locomotive Societies. After clearing Ordsall Lane No 1 signal box, the train proceeded via Castlefield Junction to the old CLC terminus at Oxford Road Station. This once more involved reversing, after which the enthusiasts enjoyed a journey via London Road South Junction, Ardwick and Midland Junctions before traversing little used lines in the Oldham and Rochdale areas. The train eventually arrived at Oldham Road Goods station where the passengers alighted - the first ones to do so for over 100 years!   **12th MAY 1956 ● PAUL SHACKCLOTH COLLECTION**

Liverpool Road Station was built at the junction of Water Street and Liverpool Road taking the line across the River Irwell into Manchester - just within the city boundary. Its continued existence is perhaps a result of its inconvenient location and when opened in 1830, the immediate area was distinctly rural. Passengers were transferred by horse bus to and from the company's office in Market Street. A similar situation existed in Liverpool. The station ceased to serve the public in 1844, at which time the Liverpool and Manchester Railway extended its line to meet the Manchester and Leeds Railway at Hunts Bank (Victoria Station) thus offering through railway connections. Liverpool Road became an important goods station and served that purpose until closure in the mid 1970's. BR English Electric diesel shunter No **D3779** stands on Water Street bridge, resting between shunting duties.

12th NOVEMBER 1962 ● GRAHAM WHITEHEAD

By 1978 the infrastructure was rapidly deteriorating and had become a target for vandals. *The Liverpool Road Station Society* in conjunction with British Rail and the Greater Manchester Council jointly addressed the problem, which resulted in funding the preservation of the buildings and the securing of the site which became earmarked for eventual use as the Manchester Museum of Science & Industry. The view at the corner of Liverpool Road and Water Street features the original Station Master's house, long since converted into shop premises. This property predated the 1830 premises by four years. The Grecian fronted former station building and offices stand adjacent. A series of twenty two brick arches running parallel with Liverpool Road carried the running lines beyond Water Street Bridge within the station area. The original warehouse facing the elevated single platform is visible, beyond which lies the former GWR Continental Warehouse, one of three built during the early LNWR period.

12th NOVEMBER 1962 ● GRAHAM WHITEHEAD

LIVERPOOL ROAD

Passing the former Liverpool Road Station building is Leyland PD2/40 No **238** working Service 70 *(Docks circular - clockwise)*. The bus is about to turn left on to Water Street before proceeding down Regent Road and Trafford Road to reach its destination. The parked estate car is standing by the doorway through which passengers wishing to travel first class once entered. A standard BR maroon sign is now affixed overhead which reads 'Liverpool Road Goods Depot General Office'. This was the official entrance for both staff and private company personnel alike making use of the facilities offered by BR.   **22nd MARCH 1969 ● P.J. THOMPSON**

Water Street Bridge looking west towards Regent Road. This is the original structure built in 1829 to carry the Liverpool and Manchester Railway into Liverpool Road Station. Pedestrians have their own right of way between the ornate pillars whilst a hood offers protection for the tram wire passing through the centre. Beyond is a second bridge which carries the line from Ordsall Lane to Castlefield Junction whilst the road junction between Water Street and Liverpool Road falls between them to the left. In August 1905 the distinctive bridge was replaced by another of a more standard pattern. *(see Page 97)*

JANUARY 1905 ● PAUL SHACKCLOTH COLLECTION

To mark the occasion, a plaque was unveiled showing that the new 'Prince's Bridge' had been jointly re-erected by the Corporations of both Manchester and Salford.

12th NOVEMBER 1962 ●
GRAHAM WHITEHEAD

Although Daimler CVG6 No 113 shows Manchester on its blinds, the bus is working the anti-clockwise Docks circular Service 71 and is in the process of turning right off Water Street into Quay Street. The onward route from Deansgate was via Blackfriars Road, Broughton Bridge, Frederick Road, Cross Lane and Trafford Road to the Docks. The Victoria and Albert Warehouses are behind the bus and date back to 1840. Improvements to the River Irwell and the Mersey into which it flows made possible the passage of ships from Liverpool. The building occupied the site of an old quay - from which Quay Street derived its name, eventually coming within the *Manchester Ship Canal Company* estate. The warehouse later became a part of the Granada complex where much of the interior happily remains as originally built.

22nd MARCH 1969 ● P.J. THOMPSON

Another view looking west down Water Street. A third bridge is now in camera, standing on which is BR Class Five 4-6-0 No **73158**. This one carried lines from Ordsall Lane Junction towards the Grape Street and Lower Byrom Street Warehouses, both of which were a part of the Liverpool Road complex. Awaiting their next instruction, the Patricroft crew are killing time by watching the world go by over the bridge parapet. A Salford bus disappears towards the Docks on Service 70 whilst a Bedford van swings right into Princes Street. The Pineapple Inn, dispensing Groves and Whitnall's ales, was an old coaching house which doubtless catered for travellers using Liverpool Road Station, just around the corner, during the period when it functioned as a passenger station between 1830 and 1844.

22nd MARCH 1966 ● TONY RENSHAW

ORDSALL LANE

The 4.30pm Llandudno 'Club' Train gets into its stride away from the city and is about to pass through the shell of Ordsall Lane Station. A regular performer was Royal Scot No **46155** *The Lancer* which had recently arrived at Llandudno Junction shed from Crewe North and was in excellent mechanical order. An unidentified Standard Class Five is in the background at the throat of Liverpool Road Goods Station.

**12th NOVEMBER 1962 ●
GRAHAM WHITEHEAD**

Ordsall Lane Station five years after closure and still remarkably intact. This forlorn view looking west along what was Platform 1 shows the Up slow line with Oldfield Road bridge in the distance. A subway connected a further four platforms but Salford's largest suburban station, like others, suffered from a lack of patronage over many years. **12th NOVEMBER 1962 ● GRAHAM WHITEHEAD**

The 80 lever Ordsall Lane No 2 Signalbox looks 'as new' having recently received long overdue attention - a legacy from the war years. This box was one of three *(Nos 1 & 4 were the others)* that outlived steam by ten years, closing on 22nd October 1978. Meanwhile a Permanent Way Gang attend to the Up Fast under the watchful eye of three signalmen. **12th NOVEMBER 1962 ● GRAHAM WHITEHEAD**

Three Car Diesel Multiple Units, later branded *Trans Pennine* and latterly Class 124, were built at Swindon in 1960 for use on accelerated Liverpool - Hull expresses via Manchester Exchange, Huddersfield and Leeds City. They were intended to run as six-car formations, and each three-car unit had two power cars, giving a six-car set 1840 bhp - a most generous power to weight ratio. The climbs from Farnley Junction to Birstall Town and from Huddersfield to Marsden could now be taken with ease. Trials took place in July 1960 after which they entered regular service on 2nd January 1961. A Hull bound six-car set is passing through the derelict Ordsall Lane platforms, having called at Earlestown only.

12th NOVEMBER 1962 ● GRAHAM WHITEHEAD

THE ROYAL TRAIN

Stanier Class Five 4-6-0 No 45290 of Bolton shed departs from Ordsall Lane Carriage Sidings with Royal Train carriages. The Reporting Number 1X00 indicates this to be an empty stock movement as distinct from the next three consecutive numbers 1X01/2 or 3 - any of which mean that Royalty is in attendance. No 45290 was the first of many Class Fives to go to Bolton in February 1962 and long serving engineman at the depot, Jim Markland, considered it to be the best they had on the books. Needless to say, the loco is in immaculate condition.

1965 ● SALFORD LOCAL HISTORY LIBRARY

A pair of Standard Class 3MT 2-6-2 tanks received at Patricroft from the Western Region, Nos **82031** and **82034** are both in unlined green, bringing a touch of colour to the sombre surroundings here.

JANUARY 1965 ● J.R. CARTER

Royal Scot 4-6-0 No 46152 *The King's Dragoon Guardsman* (6J) is passing the west end of Ordsall Lane carriage sidings with a through train for Holyhead. This point was also the throat of the former LNWR shed at Ordsall Lane (to the right), now occupied by Duncan Street Sidings.

1964 ● SALFORD LOCAL HISTORY LIBRARY

ORDSALL LANE
ENGINE SHED

When the Liverpool and Manchester Railway began through running to Victoria Station in 1844, the facilities at Ordsall Lane were less than adequate. An *1848 Ordnance Survey Map* reveals a pair of two-lane engine sheds straddling Greengate, immediately west of Victoria at a higher level. Loco use apparently ceased in 1860, at which time they became carriage sheds until the site was occupied by the building of Exchange Station (opened June 1884). In 1874 the LNWR built an 8-road shed to the standard Ramsbottom design with 2 hipped roofs, capable of accommodating 24 locos under cover. It was situated on the South side of the main line west of Ordsall Lane Station off Duncan Street. This building replaced two smaller ones dating from c.1848, the bigger of which was of four roads. When the first part of Patricroft shed opened in January 1885, Ordsall Lane became a sub-shed, but retained its own allocation and was awarded shed code No 36 in June 1892 by the LNWR. It officially closed on 20th June 1904 when Patricroft further developed its facilities. LNWR 'Problem' Class 2-2-2 No **1434 *Eunomia*** stands resplendent outside the shed. The 'Problems' were introduced by John Ramsbottom in 1859. At this time, a system of engine cleaning adopted at all LNWR sheds had to be strictly adhered to. The main frames, wheels and motion, for example, had to have all the thick grease removed by cloth or scraper before cleaning oil was applied and wiped off dry. The remainder of the engine met far more stringent requirements. *Eunomia* was withdrawn in October 1907.　　**c.1890 ● ALLAN SOMMERFIELD COLLECTION**

Webb 'Precursor' Class 2-4-0 No 1144 *Druid*, built at Crewe in 1874, stands in the shed yard. A feature of many early shed scenes were the loco crew posing from their footplate for the camera. The allocation of Passenger Tender Engines on 30th June 1896 was as follows:

1 - 7'6" Problem　　1 - 6' Whitworth
6 - Renewed Precedents

The roof of Ordsall Lane signalbox, one of the many in the area, is visible behind the men. Immediately right of the loco beyond the running lines lies the Bridgewater Greater Coal Wharf.

c.1890 ● A. HAYNES COLLECTION

Stabled in the former cattle dock at Cross Lane is an ex-L&Y Brake 56ft 3rd coach which survived in revenue earning service until the late 1950's. This example then passed into Departmental Stock and was converted into an Engineer's Department Messing Coach. This involved the removal of compartments, fixtures and fittings before being divided into workshop and messroom area. Wooden lockers and a long table positioned centrally were then installed. Lighting was by means of paraffin tilley lamps and a coal stove was provided in each section. A favoured type were the cast iron 'Empress' pattern which had a sizeable oven and integral water tank. Hand washing was confined to a galvanised bucket drawing hot water off the tank, using copious portions of 'Grimo' soap (an amalgam of crude soap and sand). The runner wagon is of LMS origin and it is likely that both vehicles were being utilised by the Manchester Civil Engineer's relaying gangs, as the wagon contains a wooden tool chest and grabs for sleepers. 25V electrification flashes had been fitted to the ends of the coach and both stovepipe chimneys had been shortened as a further precaution for 'going under the wires'. The Cattle Dock signalbox (closed 12th December 1971) and the aptly named 'London and North Western Hotel' on Cross Lane, dispensing locally brewed Threlfalls ales, are other prominent features.

DECEMBER 1965 ● R.S. GREENWOOD

CROSS LANE STATION

In the early pioneering days of the Liverpool and Manchester Railway, a station, or more correctly a stopping place, was situated here. It was known as Cross Lane Bridge and similar *stopping places* could be found at Weaste Lane, Eccles and Patricroft where the Bridgewater Canal passed under. This view is towards Manchester from the platform serving the Up Slow line and single bay -a year after the station's closure. The island platforms *(just in view on the right)* and that serving the Up Fast were staggered here. Egerton Ironworks are to the right whilst Cross Lane Cattle Sidings are to the left, out of view. Beyond Windsor Street Bridge were Salford Gasworks on either side of the line, both of which were rail connected. The Territorial Army - based at the nearby Cross Lane Barracks, departed from the station for summer camps for many years. It closed to passengers in 1959.   **1960** ● **SALFORD LOCAL HISTORY LIBRARY**

Stanier 8F 2-8-0 No 48553 brings an Up train of iron rods loaded and chained on to bogie bolster wagons between Windsor Street and Great Egerton Street bridges. The line behind the engine is designated Up and Down Goods and serves the cattle docks which are situated on the north side of the line immediately beyond the overbridge. The signals protecting it are in view over the loco's top feed and are controlled by Cross Lane Cattle Dock Signalbox, the one nearest the engine being slotted with Ordsall Lane No 4 Signalbox. The complex of pipework lies within Liverpool Road gasworks.

1st SEPTEMBER 1965 ● **GRAHAM WHITEHEAD**

A short distance down the line was Seedley Station. The distinctive wooden building and name overlooked a small station yard just off Langworthy Road on the north side of the bridge. Presumably the two men represent the station staff and the young boy a mere onlooker. A footbridge provided access to all four platforms before closure to both passenger and parcel traffic on 2nd January 1956.   **c.1900** ● **ALLAN SOMMERFIELD COLLECTION**

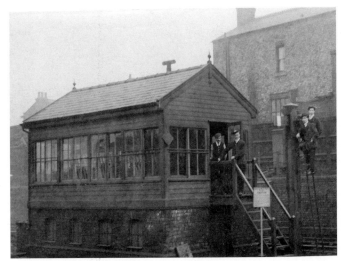

A rare photograh of Weaste Signalbox once situated west of the Station between the Down Slow and Up Fast lines. The signal is an early LNW 'Slotted Post' variety where the arm pivot is situated within the post. Weaste Station itself closed in 1948 and was demolished six years later. It had closed previously in 1942 as a wartime measure owing to a shortage of manpower, but the box went long before the war.   **c.1920** ● **JOHN RYAN COLLECTION**

Approaching the junction with Regent Road is Salford Car No **339** on Service 34 to Weaste. It was renumbered in 1935 from No 110, which was new in 1903 as an open-top vestibuled bogie car built by G.F. Milnes. A vestibuled top cover was supplied by Brush in 1925. Car No **222** *(right)* has just crossed the junction and is on its way to Manchester on Service 71. The disused track in the foreground was the former route to the Docks and Trafford Park via Ordsall Lane.

10th AUGUST 1939 ● W.A. CAMWELL

CROSS LANE

Thirty years later and two Daimler CVG6 buses are passing at the busy Cross Lane/ Regent Road junction. No **513** is returning from Trafford Park to Manchester (Bridge Street) on Service 84 whilst No **526** is indicating to turn right on its journey to Eccles, via Eccles New Road and Weaste on Service 54. Though most of Salford's post war buses were Daimlers, they all carried Gardner engines as specified by the Transport Department. The last six in the replacement programme, Nos 555-560 had heater units and were usually employed on the all night services operating from Victoria Bus Station. One of these typical post-war Salford buses, No 511, is preserved in the Tameside Transport Collection at Roaches (near Mossley). The Cross Lane branch of Williams Deacons Bank Ltd is prominent on the corner and the name, long since defunct, is often locally associated with Jubilee 4-6-0 No 45596 *Bahamas,* as certain senior officials were involved in securing the loco's preservation.

5th APRIL 1969 ● P.J. THOMPSON

Salford Cars Nos 372 and 159 stand on Eccles New Road at Weaste awaiting departure. No 159 was built by Brush of Loughborough with Westinghouse motors and Brill trucks. Introduced into service in 1914 and withdrawn in August 1939, it was about to travel to Trafford Park with a workmen's special during the rush hour. Car No 372 was an odd-one-out, in that it was given a non-standard vestibule in an attempt to show that management was doing something about the crews' complaints of working on open-platform cars in cold weather. But Salford being Salford, the programme was halted after a brief flirtation. The excuse was that some drivers said that side draughts experienced on vestibuled cars were worse than being out in the open. It is working the former joint service No 34, originally Belle Vue to Weaste but cut back to run only from Deansgate to Weaste in July 1937. As a result, it was operated solely by Salford cars at this time.

28th JULY 1938 ● W.A. CAMWELL

Just beyond Weaste Garage off Eccles New Road was Ariel Street lay-by, the terminus for the Weaste bus services. Three members of Salford's fleet are congregated here - each one in typically spotless condition with radiator cowls shining. This, despite a polluted atmosphere - the result of heavy local industry. By 1950, SCT buses had become the envy of many a transport manager. There was a strong argument that Salford had the finest municipal fleet in the country - and few would disagree. The buses identified are No **289**, a Leyland PD1 with Metro-Cammell bodywork on Service 76 (Weaste to Manchester, King Street West). No **302**, another Leyland PD1, but with Leyland bodywork working Service 1 (Weaste to Mandley Park). In post-war years, Service 76 lasted until September 1952, when it was replaced by circular services 44/54.

c.1950 ● J. FOZARD

BARTON LANE AQUEDUCT

Passing under Barton Lane Aqueduct, which carries the Bridgewater Canal is No **444**, a Daimler CVG6 with Burlingham bodywork. It is returning to the City from Peel Green on Service 5 which, as mentioned on page 34, had to be operated by single deck buses because of this low 11ft. 9ins. bridge. This was Salford's only concern. Other services which passed under the notorious bridge were Lancashire United Transport's No 41 between Eccles and Bolton and Services 87/88 between Eccles and Trafford Park. Others were the jointly operated Service 22 - the preserve of Manchester Corporation and North Western Road Car (see Page 112) and Service 107 between Eccles and Flixton, the preserve of N.W.R.C. Passing in the opposite direction is a black taxi cab, registration LVM 502, whose white plate shows *Manchester Hackney Carriage No 63*.

c.1959 ● DAVID YOUNG COLLECTION

WEASTE DEPOT

The Weaste Omnibus Depot was formally opened on 29th October 1929 to house a part of the ever growing fleet of buses, all of which could not be accommodated at Frederick Road. The building, which faced on to Eccles Old Road, was of irregular shape, determined by the maximum use of land bounded by Weaste Road South, Hessel Street and Humber Street, and housed 80 buses and 25 trams from the outset. Ex-Salford Leyland PD2/40 No 157, which has already acquired its SELNEC fleet number of **3008**, is ready to leave whilst nearby are two unidentified rear-engined buses already carrying the new livery. The clock tower at the Eccles end of the building was a familiar local landmark.

12th MAY 1974 ● ALLAN SOMMERFIELD

The depot also provided accommodation for a small number of trams, which gained entrance by passing down Weaste Road South at the side of the building and into Hessel Street. The two entrances led directly on to a traverser which positioned the cars on nine parallel tracks. They left by the front entrance on to Eccles New Road. The original tracks remained in-situ behind the depot on Hessel Street long after the trams' demise, acting as a reminder to the long suffering residents who lived in such close proximity.

1972 ● ALLAN SOMMERFIELD

Maintaining the high standards of appearance set by Mr Baroth, a member of the maintenance staff hoses down 7' 6" Daimler No **455** which has just arrived back at the depot. The Transport Committee coach, ERJ 451 is also visible.

1961 ● THE OMNIBUS SOCIETY

Reverse liveried Daimler CVG6 No 469 has just pulled out of Weaste Garage prior to heading for Mandley Park on Service 1. Seeking uniformity, General Manager Charles Baroth embarked on a major fleet renewal programme which resulted in the delivery of 195 of these vehicles, all of which had Metro-Cammell bodies. They were delivered between 1950 and 1952 bringing Salford City Transport to the forefront among public transport undertakings. By February 1952, they had 304 buses in service operated by a staff of 1,571 men and women which included administration and service engineers.

1961 ● DAVID YOUNG COLLECTION

MANCHESTER SHIP CANAL BRANCH

The Manchester Ship Canal Branch from Eccles to Weaste Junction opened for traffic on 4th November 1895. The rival L&YR, whose branch from Windsor Bridge to New Barns Junction was largely through tunnel, opened nearly three years later. The 'Lanky' worked their trains by arrangement and had running powers during the interim period. The double track line fell away before passing under the main line and Eccles New Road before reaching the Exchange Sidings, north of Weaste Junction. The branch also offered connections to the Mode Wheel Sewage Works, Ship Canal Tar Works and the Northern Creosoting Company, where railway sleepers and telegraph poles were treated. Standard Class Five No **73069** has no problem with the gradient, returning from the Exchange Sidings, having deposited its train.

SEPTEMBER 1967 ● BERNARD CRICK

Reduced to mundane work, Jubilee Class 4-6-0 No **45563** *Australia* blows off steam whilst propelling its train of mixed goods wagons down the gradient towards Weaste Exchange Sidings. The line was singled just after the end of steam on 7th October 1968 when Weaste Junction became a casualty to general traffic - the Lancashire tar distillers oil trains used the line for a period but it remains open for traffic to the Blue Circle Cement Terminal. In earlier days, Patricroft had employed ex-LNW 0-8-2 tank engines on the branch for many years.

JULY 1961 ● J.R. CARTER

STOTT LANE SIDINGS

Stott Lane Exchange Sidings were the focal point for incoming goods trains bound for the docks. The wagons were marshalled within the eleven roads available before proceeding the short distance to Weaste. Caprotti Standard Class Five No **73125** is engaged on such work with the shunter adopting a familiar pose, clinging on to the cab handrail before re-setting the points. Many of the Patricroft enginemen disliked these Caprotti engines, claiming they were often 'found wanting' on the Yorkshire trains on the climb to Standedge and couldn't keep time. The Chester and North Wales turns presented no such problems. Of the 172 locos built, Patricroft had an association with 58 members of the BR Standard Class Five at some stage in their life. Five examples survive in preservation, three of which, Nos 73050, 73096 and Caprotti No 73129 were withdrawn from the shed.

SEPTEMBER 1967 ● BERNARD CRICK

A busy scene east of Eccles. Standard Class Five No **73050** is working tender first on the Up Fast with a hopper train and passes an unidentified English Electric Type 4 Diesel on the Down Slow, again with a loaded mineral train but composed of standard BR 16-ton mineral wagons. Sister engine No **73069**, in much better external condition, stands at the neck of Stott Lane Sidings. Both Standards were Patricroft locos but the latter was transferred to Carnforth for a final fling upon the shed's closure on 1st July 1968. It had appeared on a number of enthusiasts' specials during the final months of steam. Note the freshly ballasted permanent way on a section of line where the water troughs were once situated.   **1967 ● BERNARD CRICK**

The view from Cock Robin Bridge off Tan Pit Lane looking east towards Ordsall Lane and Manchester. The water troughs had been laid here in 1876 by the LNW Railway and lasted until the early 1960's. The original troughs dating back to 1861, were situated at Parkside, near Earlestown, but an overburdening demand on the local water supply resulted in their transfer. Eccles also had the advantage of serving the Monton line, and apparently the Leeds area ultimately benefited with the saving of water at Stalybridge. The Down Slow was 556 yards long whilst the other three running lines were 50 yards shorter. The junction for the *Manchester Ship Canal branch* is in the left foreground beyond which lie Stott Lane Sidings, once overlooked by *The Homestead* - a block of old people's homes behind Hope Hospital.

MARCH 1960 ● SALFORD LOCAL HISTORY LIBRARY

ECCLES TROUGHS

Forging through Eccles towards Manchester and about to run over the water troughs is ex-LMS 4F 0-6-0 No **44599** with a train of stone empties from Atherton to Burton. As many as 580 locos in the class were taken into BR stock in 1948. They were introduced in 1924 and were a post-grouping development of the Midland design with reduced boiler mountings. This example, allocated to Burton, is attached to a high-sided tender which it received on entering service in 1940. Another six engines were similarly attached (Nos 4578/87/94/96, 4601/2) but only ten examples of the 3,500 gallon Fowler tender were built in the early Stanier days, and were originally coupled to Crewe built Jubilees. They had increased capacity and required no coal rails. The remaining three apparently led more nomadic lives and were frequently exchanged between a variety of engines. These locos were most prominent at work over the ex-Midland lines, but examples were widely scattered and about thirty could be found in Scotland. **JUNE 1961** ● **J.R. CARTER**

Two moving trains passing each other within camera shot was a rare occurrence. Photographer Wilf Cooper had positioned himself on Cock Robin Bridge primarily to record Royal Scot 4-6-0 No **46144** *Honourable Artillery Company* (6G) approaching Eccles on the Up Fast with a North Wales express. The Standard Class Five coming into view with an eastbound parcels train is a bonus, resulting in a nicely composed photograph. Behind the ex-LNER Gresley full brake stands the water softening plant for the nearby Eccles troughs. **JUNE 1962** ● **W.D. COOPER**

ECCLES STATION

Eccles Station looking West. The connection in the foreground between Fast and Slow running lines immediately east of the station was the scene of a serious accident. The disaster occurred on the morning of Tuesday, 30th December 1941 at 8.18am when two crowded passenger trains collided, resulting in 23 fatalities and 56 seriously injured. Both trains had, coincidentally, departed at 6.53am. A stopping train from Kenyon Junction to Manchester Exchange via Tyldesley was hauled by Stanier 2-6-2T No 203 whilst a workmen's train from Rochdale to Pennington (between Leigh and Kenyon Junction) and not included in the public timetable, had Fowler 2-6-4T No 2406 in charge. Conditions were extremely foggy and delays all over the system were being encountered. After stopping at Eccles Station, the Manchester bound train was transferring from Up Slow to Up Fast as No 2406 approached on the Down Slow at 30mph striking the leading coach on the crossover. As the incident happened during wartime, it remained one of the least publicised and, as a consequence, least known about in railway history. A deep gouge in the retaining wall remained unattended, acting as a memorial to those who were aware of the tragedy.

OCTOBER 1959 ● SALFORD LOCAL HISTORY LIBRARY

A Newton Heath Class Five, No 44891 transfers from the Down Fast to Down Slow in readiness to take the Monton line at Eccles Junction. The train is the 3.59pm Manchester Victoria to Barrow, routed via Ellenbrook and Springs Branch Junction, Wigan then on to Preston up the West Coast Main Line. After 1960, the 'Barrer' worked over ex-L&Y metals, travelling via Bolton Trinity Street and Chorley before reaching Preston. The Up Fast Starter at the platform end is an LMS restricted clearance signal, whilst between signal and engine is a pre-cast chipping bin originating from Newton Heath Concrete Works, specimens of which could always be seen at regular intervals alongside the permanent way.

1956 ● W.D. COOPER

Rebuilt Patriot No 45527 *Southport* bursts through Platform 2 with the 9.00am Liverpool Lime Street to Newcastle Express. Carmine and cream liveried Mark 1 corridor coaching stock was still the order of the day on principal passenger trains whilst all-crimson coaches were found on most local stopping trains. The crew of Stanier 8F No **48320** take interest in its passage whilst idling away time awaiting the signal before proceeding to Patricroft shed for servicing. Their freight loco is a stranger, coming from Nuneaton (2B).

1957 ● W.D. COOPER

This trio of photographs of Eccles Station reveals that little has changed over the years, which saw it pass from LNWR, LMS and finally into BR ownership. It was originally classified as a 'Halt' on the Liverpool to Manchester Railway but improved in status on becoming a part of the LNWR in 1846. The opening of the line to Monton and beyond in 1883 resulted in the quadrupling of tracks and development of the facilities here. The wooden station building provided the usual facilities and access to all four platforms was via a footbridge. Elliotts Sweet Shop occupied a part of the building as did a branch of Coop and Sons, Funeral Directors, whose head office was at Pendleton. The Station Cigar Stores are also present on the right. Salford open top Car No **75** is about to pass down Gilda Brook Road in the direction of Hope Hospital. Electric tramcars replaced horse trams on the Eccles Old Road route in 1902.   **c.1904** ● **SALFORD LOCAL HISTORY LIBRARY**

Religion played a large part in the lives of many Eccles inhabitants. In the Victorian and Edwardian periods, all Sunday Schools took part in Whit or Anniversary Walks as annual events. With everyone attired in their 'Sunday Best', a typical gathering of people are about to pass down Wellington Road on the occasion of the '1888 - 1938 Golden Jubilee'. Such traditions were maintained throughout the days of steam and beyond, although it was always an activity much preferred by young girls. These walks were a favourite subject with commercial photographers who were able to sell prints to the participants afterwards. The shops within the station, now owned by the LMS, have changed hands. The Cigar Stores now occupy the former funeral directors and James E Owen, Estate Agents and Valuers has the old sweet shop, whilst a new firm Samuel Hooley and Sons are also present.

1938 ● **SALFORD LOCAL HISTORY LIBRARY**

Twenty years on and into the BR era. A third sign now adorns the station building over the entrance and the shops appear to remain in business. The stone setts have long since disappeared and a traffic island directing motorists to 'keep left' is the order of the day. Further down Church Road on the right once stood *Ye Olde Thatche*, the original Eccles Cake shop supposedly built as long ago as 1094, but unfortunately demolished in 1915 during World War 1. Passengers queue to board Leyland PD1A No **329** which is working Service 66 to Peel Green. The vehicle carries the standard green and cream livery with silver roof. A small green enamel plate with the wording 'Salford City Transport' is affixed to the top of the highly polished radiator cowl, as was the case with all buses within the fleet.

1958 ●
SALFORD LOCAL HISTORY LIBRARY

A serious collision in August 1961 near Warrington Dallam shed resulted in the blocking of the West Coast Main line in the area for a twenty four hour period. The locomotives involved were Jubilee 4-6-0 No 45630 *Swaziland* which was coming off shed and Stanier Class Five No 45401, heading a southbound freight from the Liverpool area. The impact was so severe that both engines were withdrawn from service. As a result, Crewe North Stanier Pacific No **46253 *City of St Albans*** had been diverted at Crewe and travelled via Wilmslow, Manchester Piccadilly and Oxford Road, Castlefield Junction and Ordsall Lane. The train is the Birmingham - Glasgow express which will shortly take the Monton line before passing through Ellenbrook and Tyldesley. The crew's lack of route knowledge beyond Manchester involved Billy Leigh from Patricroft, acting as Pilotman between Manchester Piccadilly (MSJ&A Platforms) and Springs Branch Junction, Wigan - where the train rejoined its original route.   **28th AUGUST 1961** ● **J.R. CARTER**

Another northbound train is in the hands of Jubilee 4-6-0 No **45586 *Mysore*.** The Aston-based loco is carrying inter-regional Reporting Number 1Z61. Photographer Jim Carter has retreated to the bridge carrying Monton Road over the line between Eccles Station and Junction. The spires of Eccles Methodist Church (foreground) and the Congregational Church (background) feature in many of the photographs taken in the Eccles vicinity.   **28th AUGUST 1961** ● **J.R. CARTER**

ECCLES BUS STATION

Salford No 294 was a Leyland PD1 with Metro-Cammell bodywork, new in 1947 and working out of Weaste Garage. The previous year, Salford City Transport adopted a new green and cream livery to differentiate from Manchester, LUT and North Western, all of which were red. The bus is on Service 54, which will return to Manchester (Bridge Street) via Clarendon Crescent, Weaste and Oldfield Road.

AUGUST 1958 ● J. FOZARD

Salford had no involvement with the jointly operated Service 22 between Levenshulme (Lloyd Road) and Eccles Bus Station. Manchester Corporation and North Western Road Car vehicles worked the 15 minute interval service which travelled by way of Withington (Mauldeth Road), Chorlton Office, Wilbraham Road, Stretford (King Street) and Urmston Station, arriving at Eccles after passing under Barton Bridge. In 1962, seven MCTD buses operated from Parrs Wood Garage and a solitary vehicle from the NWRC depot at Urmston. In addition, some short workings ran as extras during the peak periods. A 1953 Leyland Royal Tiger with Northern Counties bodywork, No **24**, is one of only two examples which had crush-loader body design to increase capacity. In December 1956 it was fitted with a heater prior to a trip to Vienna, although ten years later both were sold for further use as internal buses at Manchester Airport. No 25 is preserved in the Manchester Transport Museum at Boyle Street. **c.1960 ● J. FOZARD**

The depths of the last big freeze. The winter of 1962/63 will be remembered by many who had to undergo the treacherous conditions under foot for weeks on end. Under the circumstances, one could forgive Salford City Transport for not keeping their vehicles in exemplary condition at the time. No **453**, a Daimler CVG6 with Burlingham bodywork, was one of a small batch of four 7' 6" wide vehicles dedicated to work on Service 6. This operated between Eccles and Radcliffe by way of the notorious Rainsough Brow - permission to use double-deck buses up the steep climb having been granted in 1951. An unusual feature at Eccles Bus Station were the cast iron supports beneath the green painted shelters. Within the angle brackets were the route details picked out in black and white.

**21st JANUARY 1963 ●
SALFORD LOCAL HISTORY LIBRARY**

Ten Atkinson buses with Gardner engines were added to the North Western fleet in 1952. Nos 500 - 509 had Weymann 42 seat bodywork and they tended to be concentrated at Urmston Depot. No **503** is on Service 107 (Eccles - Davyhulme - Flixton, Carrington Road). The forerunner in the series (No 500) is under restoration at a private site in the Macclesfield area. Behind stands No **523**, an Atkinson Alpha single-deck with Roe bodywork, new to Lancashire United Transport in 1954. It is on Service 87 (Eccles - Trafford Park via Barton Bridge) which was solely operated by LUT. Both these services passed under the Bridgewater Canal, so that single-deck operation was essential. The Eccles, or Lane End Bus Station as it was also known by, opened in 1938 offering improved facilities as well as relieving congestion on the busy main road.

1956 ● ABCROSS

ECCLES JUNCTION

The Salford - Carlisle Goods left Liverpool Road Station on Monday to Friday at 7.05pm and was a favourite train of photographer Wilf Cooper who recorded it on numerous occasions. His lineside pass enabled him to achieve dramatic trackside level images such as the three examples featured here. The train was diagrammed for a Carlisle Upperby engine and this early view features unrebuilt Patriot No **45524 Blackpool** carrying a 12A shedplate, dating the photo between January 1955 and February 1958. The lamp positions unusually indicate a Class 'D' train, a fitted freight on this occasion.

c.1956 ● W.D. COOPER

THE CARLISLE GOODS

A member of the rebuilt variety of Patriot - No 45526 Morecambe and Heysham. When the former Caledonian shed at Carlisle Kingmoor came under LMR control in February 1958, the ex-LNWR establishment at Upperby reverted to 12B. This loco was one of two long standing rebuilt Patriots at the shed which carried both shed plates, the other being No 45512 Bunsen which had the distinction of working the last steam hauled fitted freight to Carlisle. A plaque commemorating the occasion can be seen near Princes Bridge which crosses Water Street carrying lines into Liverpool Road Goods Station.

c.1960 ● W.D. COOPER

The first numerical member of the Jubilee Class, No 45552 Silver Jubilee appeared on the train on several occasions in the 1950's when it was one of several allocated to Upperby. By the Spring of 1962 it was a Crewe North engine and had pre-sumably been borrowed on this occasion. The loco is carrying the usual Class 'C' headlamps, indicating that the train is 'fully fitted', being composed of vacuum-braked stock connected to the engine. Note the splitting signals which are now sited east of Monton Road bridge and would have resulted in improved sighting for the enginemen. The earlier lower quadrant variety are present in the first photograph.

MAY 1962 ● W.D. COOPER

Eccles Junction looking in the Manchester direction from 'Four Bridges'. The Monton main (or goods) lines pass directly under whilst the lines to Liverpool are to the right, behind Eccles Junction signalbox, which had no control of the Up and Down Fast between Patricroft Station and Eccles boxes. The local coal yard once occupied the ground behind the train of hopper wagons whilst St Andrew's Church is another substantial religious establishment within the Borough of Eccles. **1968 ● STATIONS UK**

One of the last suburban trains between Manchester Exchange and Wigan North Western takes the Monton line at Eccles Junction. Stanier Class 4MT 2-6-4T No **42474** (9H) and three coaches has just passed under the footbridge which offered public access to Wellington Road on the north side from a footpath between Bright Road and Devonshire Road which ran alongside the railway *(see below)*. It was known locally as 'Four Bridges' and was a popular haunt for trainspotters as it overlooked the new shed and sidings as well as the main running lines. In the early 1960's, a mongrel dog, who obviously lived locally, took great delight in patrolling this footbridge. He also sensed the approach of an engine and would stand directly over the line, shrouded in steam, whilst awaiting the next one!

OCTOBER 1964 ● W.D. COOPER

The 'Swindon' influence brought to the LMS by Sir William Stanier was first apparent in these locos brought into service in 1933. The tapered boiler and dome flanked with top-feed pipes and fittings were common features found on many GWR locos. The class of 40, often referred to as 'Stanier Crabs', were originally rated 5P/4F and were designed for use on heavy excursion trains in addition to fast freight work. They were to be found working over the former LNWR system, mainly in the north and this example, No **2971** belonged to Speke Junction. The engine appears to be in ex-works condition and is seen passing Patricroft Sidings, light engine, heading in the direction of Liverpool.

17th MAY 1945 ● W.D. COOPER

On a cold winter's morning, an express train for North Wales roars past Patricroft Sidings signalbox, between Eccles Junction and Patricroft Station, headed by the first Standard Class Five with Caprotti valve-gear, No **73125.** The following 29 locos were similarly treated but the class as a whole (172 members) always lived within the shadow of the Stanier 5MT's, although their purpose was to replace older 4-6-0's and 4P 4-4-0's. They operated on the main lines of all regions with many being found on the ex-Midland lines and in the Glasgow area. No 73125 lasted until the end, being withdrawn from Patricroft Shed upon its closure on 1st July 1968. Local enthusiast and photographer Ian Cockcroft had braved the snow underfoot to record this dramatic lineside view.

DECEMBER 1962 ● IAN COCKCROFT

The Midland Railway never had anything larger than a 4-4-0 for passenger work and the tradition stuck fast. After the Grouping, Sir Henry Fowler produced new designs for 4-4-0's along similar lines. He introduced two varieties, the larger was the celebrated 4P LMS 'Compound' Class, first introduced in 1924 and the smaller, which had two inside cylinders and rated at 2P, went into traffic four years later. They were numbered 40563 - 40700 and could be found scattered over most parts of the LMS system. Many were in Scotland, principally in the Kilmarnock area but others could be found in the deep south on the Somerset and Dorset Joint system. In 1948, Rhyl depot on the North Wales coast had three examples, Nos M629, M671/5. Here in early BR days, carrying its short lived number, No M671 passes Eccles Junction with a stopping train to Chester. The engine found its way on to Patricroft's allocation in March 1957. The distinctive building beside Monton Road Bridge is the Eccles Conservative Club.

OCTOBER 1948 ● W.D. COOPER

An unusual view through the wire mesh which lined the 'Four Bridges' foot-bridge. The loco is none other than the double chimneyed Jubilee 4-6-0 destined for preservation, No **45596** *Bahamas.* It is on the Up Goods line approaching Eccles Junction from the Monton direction and displaying a single headlamp above the bufferbeam indicating a 'Branch Line Freight Train'. Stockport Edgeley engines were regular visitors to the area, but this particular loco was on familiar territory, being based at Edge Hill and Carlisle Upperby during the 1950's. By 1966, Jubilees were becoming an endangered species and *Bahamas* only had another five months left in service. George Davies, Manager of the Longsight branch of Williams Deacons Bank expressed an early interest in No 45596's survival and the rest, as they say, is history.

**FEBRUARY 1966 ●
SALFORD LOCAL HISTORY LIBRARY**

The Liverpool to Newcastle service switched to diesel traction in January 1961 at the same time as the commencement of the newly introduced Trans Pennine service to Hull. The multiple units were also considered for this route but the longer formations which would have been needed were deemed uneconomical. Main line diesels based at Gateshead and Edge Hill worked the trains throughout and the stock was composed of a nine coach Standard Mark 1 formation including a restaurant car. The last member of the Type 4 'Peak' Class of Diesel Electric locomotives, No **D193,** based on Tyneside, eases its train towards Liverpool past Eccles Junction signalbox.

JULY 1961 ● IAN COCKCROFT

'Jinty' 0-6-0 No 47365 is going about its business transferring half a dozen empty mineral wagons in the vicinity of Patricroft Sidings. Three more wagons stand scattered within the coal yard behind Eccles Junction Signalbox.

18TH APRIL 1962 ● B.W.L. BROOKSBANK

Another Gateshead 'Peak', No D187 passes in the other direction, returning home with a Newcastle train. On this occasion the diesel is displaying a pair of traditional headlamps in the 'Class A' position, signifying 'Express Passenger Train', rather than making use of the headcode panel provided at either end of the locomotive. Also in view is Patricroft Sidings, a 58 lever signalbox, a short distance west of Eccles Junction.

JULY 1961 ● IAN COCKCROFT

PATRICROFT SIDINGS

Patricroft enginemen had a habit of nicknaming one or two of their 'Jinties'. The name *Tivvy* has been neatly applied to the tank sides of No **47662** by the shed scribe. The engine is acting as Yard Pilot, hastily substituting for a failed six-coupled diesel shunter. An unidentified 8F standing on the Up Monton Loop line is blowing off steam, probably awaiting clearance to go on shed. Another member is fronting on to the original LNWR coaling stage with water tank over the top. A similar building survived in the new shed yard. A handful of locos in steam was all that could be found in the vicinity at certain times of day as the empty shed yard clearly testifies.

OCTOBER 1965 ●
SALFORD LOCAL HISTORY LIBRARY

A candidate for the most travelled ex-L&Y 'A' Class locomotive in the LMS and BR period must be 0-6-0 No **52201**. The loco's whereabouts in L&Y days (as No 437) are obscure, but immediately prior to the Grouping in 1921 it was at Wakefield. Its next known allocation was Newton Heath in 1932 and from that time onwards the list makes for interesting reading:

April 1936 - **Stoke**	July 1955 - **Nuneaton**
November 1936 - **Bolton**	November 1957 - **Sutton Oak**
December 1936 - **Springs Branch**	February 1958 - **Crewe South**
January 1945 - **Carlisle Upperby**	April 1958 - **Crewe Works**
July 1946 - **Moor Row**	July 1958 - **Patricroft**
August 1954 - **Workington**	August 1959 - **Bury**

Withdrawn from Bury in February 1961.

No 52201 was on Patricroft's allocation at the time of the photograph, despite carrying a Sutton Oak (10D) shedplate.

AUGUST 1958 ● **P.H. GROOM**

Stanier 'Crab' 2-6-0 No 42978 moves a 'Class H' through freight out of Patricroft Sidings. These engines weren't uncommon in the area - Springs Branch, Wigan had a few, but many of the 40 members were concentrated at Aston and Crewe South sheds, although they could also be found at Mold Junction and Birkenhead. Notice the ex-LNER B1 4-6-0 in the 'new' shed yard. **1965** ● **SALFORD LOCAL HISTORY LIBRARY**

Another Stockport Edgeley loco, No 44445 passes through, light engine towards Eccles Junction on the Up main line. Despite being widely allocated, the Fowler 4F 0-6-0 Class never appeared carrying 10C or 26F shedplates. However, a Midland example, No 43976 arrived in October 1959 from Accrington for a short period before moving on to Lower Darwen in February 1960. No 44445 was withdrawn in June 1963.

1962 ● SALFORD LOCAL HISTORY LIBRARY

A lengthy parcels train arrives from the Liverpool direction headed by an unidentified Stanier 8F 2-8-0. Between the main line and Patricroft shed were extensive sidings which dealt with goods traffic in each direction. Immediately behind the train were the Down Liverpool Goods 1 & 2 followed by 6 sorting sidings. Between the Up Through and Arrivals tracks were Brindle (7) and Jubilee (3) Sidings. **JUNE 1961 ● IAN COCKCROFT**

A heavy ground frost helps to highlight the complexity of the Permanent Way at the west end neck of the yard. An unidentified Standard Class Five 4-6-0 rolls a freight under the footbridge leading to the shed and is taking the Up through road. A Jubilee 4-6-0 is up against the signal, awaiting the 'off' in the other direction with a hopper train. About to take coal under the plant is a Stanier 8F 2-8-0, complete with a Fowler tender. **DECEMBER 1962 ● IAN COCKCROFT**

A Farnley Junction Class Five 4-6-0, No 45079 is deputising for the Jubilee usually provided by that depot from Leeds City with the cross-country Restaurant Car express from Newcastle to Liverpool Lime Street. The route of certain trains from Newcastle to Leeds left the East Coast Main Line at Northallerton and went by way of Melmerby, Ripon and Harrogate. Ex-LNER Pacifics from Heaton, Gateshead and Leeds, Neville Hill were regular performers over this section. After the Ripon route closed in March 1967, these trains used the main line via York instead. No 45079 will call at Earlestown (for Warrington and St. Helens Shaw Street) only. I wonder how many trainspotters lived on Hampden Grove? The views from the bedroom windows can only be imagined!

1953 ● W.D. COOPER

Another Liverpool bound express is in the hands of Rebuilt Royal Scot 4-6-0 No **46139 *The Welch Regiment*.** The engine is from Camden and has possibly been borrowed by Edge Hill for the working. Along with other members, it was ousted from the Euston services in September 1959 by an influx of Type 4 main line diesels. No 46139 made the short move to Kentish Town where it worked on the Midland Main Line for a further two years. A similar pattern emerged at St. Pancras and the engine came north to Newton Heath in September 1961, its final resting place.

MARCH 1959 ● W.D. COOPER

The 4-6-0 Jubilee class also suffered in a similar manner. No **45638 *Zanzibar*** was a familiar engine in the city, operating out of Longsight Depot, originally as No 5638, since 1943. A combination of dieselisation and electrification resulted in its departure at the end of the 1960 Summer Timetable. After a spell near the coast at Llandudno Junction, No 45638 went to Warrington Dallam in October 1961 along with former 'Royal Train' engine No 45671 *Prince Rupert*, which had followed in its path. Although situated on the West Coast Main line, Dallam had no express passenger diagrams and these two, together with Nos 45583 *Assam* and 45655 *Keith* were the first of the class to be allocated - almost exclusively for freight work. *Zanzibar* leaves the sidings working towards it's home town with a mixed goods train. The loco is in unlined green for reasons of economy but the front numberplate appears to have received special treatment.

JUNE 1963 ● W.D. COOPER

The only Patricroft engine that was motor fitted for pull and push working in early BR days was Ivatt Class 2MT 2-6-2T No **41287.** It arrived in October 1954 specifically to work the Tyldesley to Leigh motor trains during the day. In addition, it also worked an early morning train from Tyldesley to Wigan North Western and return, as well as an evening Tyldesley to Earlestown motor train. The loco shunted at Leigh in the mornings. It was joined by another, No 41283 from Fleetwood in December 1959, but both moved away on to the Southern Region in June 1961, firstly to Brighton, then Guildford and Eastleigh in the case of No 41287. The 'motor train' turn was popular with the enginemen as many considered these engines the most comfortable to work on. The tapered central coal bunker had a three ton capacity, offering excellent visibility to the rear for backward running as can be seen. The engine is passing Patricroft Station signalbox before retiring to the shed. **1955 ● W.D. COOPER**

Another Jubilee hard at work is No 45711 *Courageous.* In September 1952 this engine moved to Corkerhill, Glasgow and in exchange Farnley Junction acquired No 45646 *Napier* in its place. *Courageous* remained north of the border until its withdrawal in 1963 and became much sought after by many young Mancunian enthusiasts, including the author. The previous generation of 'gricers' had no such problems underlining its name and number as it was a Newton Heath engine in LMS days. A new 00 scale model of this Jubilee is on the market, nicely finished in lined black livery and is accurate to the minutest detail - except for the shed code which shows 55A. *Courageous* was never a Leeds Holbeck engine! **JULY 1951 ● W.D. COOPER**

Lodging Houses (or Barracks) existed at many of the principal depots and upon Nationalisation, 43 permanent staff hostels were scattered over the former LMS region. Patricroft, like the vast majority of others, suffered from a lack of investment over the years and a building that once housed 40 beds during the LNWR period had 61 by 1948, although there is no record regarding any extension to the premises. They were often situated adjacent to, or within the shed yards which was hardly conducive to a good night's (or day's) sleep. Patricroft's facilities were perhaps even worse as the barracks were next to the main line at the east end of the station, on a stretch where the engines are 'opening up' for the race across Chat Moss, whilst the Manchester-bound trains were often braking hard for the signal checks on the approach to Eccles Junction. Jubilee 4-6-0 No **45646 *Napier*** picks up speed outside the bedroom windows with a Liverpool train. **JULY 1961 ● W.D. COOPER**

Many of the Chester locals in the early 1950's were in the hands of that depots ex-LMS Compound 4-4-0's. A young trainspotter sat on the wall takes a careful note of No **41157** which makes a fine sight passing Patricroft Station Signalbox. This engine, in fully lined black livery, was to become one of the last left in service. It moved on to Trafford Park in December 1957 before going to Derby in January 1959 and was withdrawn from there in May 1960. Three more trainspotters are trudging across the footbridge and appear to show little interest in the passing train. They might have fallen victim to the 'gaffer' on shed and been told, in no uncertain terms, to leave the premises.

JUNE 1955 ● W.D. COOPER

No 45530
SIR FRANK REE

This locomotive was built in April 1933 at Crewe and numbered 6022 (the number carried by the 'Claughton' 4-6-0 which it replaced). It was re-numbered 5530 in August 1934 and again after Nationalisation in April 1948, becoming No 45530 during which time it had become the first 'Patriot' to be rebuilt (October 1946). As No 5530 it was not the first 'Patriot' to be named Sir Frank Ree. The second member of the class, No 5902, built at Derby in November 1930, carried the name until 1937 when it became St. Dunstans (re-numbered 5501 in April 1934). No 5530 then assumed the name Sir Frank Ree, having previously run nameless. The engine went new to Patricroft shed where it stayed until 4th January 1936. (Other members, Nos 5524/9/31 also went new there but did not stay long). Its subsequent allocation history is as follows:

4th Jan 1936 - **Camden**	17th Apr 1948 - **Leeds Holbeck**	10th June 1961 - **Willesden**
20th Feb 1937 - **Crewe North**	15th May 1948 - **Longsight**	23rd Sept 1961 - **Llandudno Jctn**
10th Apr 1937 - **Camden**	25th Apr 1959 - **Trafford Park**	7th July 1962 - **Willesden**
10th Feb 1940 - **Crewe North**	13th June 1959 - **Longsight**	June 1964 - **Holyhead**
5th Apr 1947 - **Longsight**	10th Sept 1960 - **Camden**	Jan 1965 - **Carlisle Kingmoor**

The Llandudno Club Train passes under the footbridge leading to Patricroft shed in the hands of No **45530 *Sir Frank Ree*** (6G). On this occasion the engine crew are conscious of photographer Wilf Cooper's presence and have 'put on a show'. The cylinder drain cocks are open as the train is about to pass through Patricroft Station - a practice much frowned upon by authority. No 45530 was the last 'Patriot' in service before being withdrawn in January 1966 after having covered 1,740,019 miles in service. **MAY 1962 ● W.D. COOPER**

Bowen-Cooke 'Prince of Wales Tank' Class 4P 4-6-2T No 6982 departs from Patricroft Station with a stopping train for Manchester Exchange. The loco is painted in plain black livery and carries the LMS coat of arms on the bunker sides, A total of 47 Pacific tanks were introduced between 1910 and 1916 and all were withdrawn between 1936 and 1941.

c.1930 ● PAUL SHACKCLOTH COLLECTION

Patricroft Station looking West. An assortment of wagons occupy the goods yard beyond which are part of the original premises of Nasmyth Wilson.

1960 ● SALFORD LOCAL HISTORY LIBRARY

Stanier 8F 2-8-0 No 48692 passes through the platforms with a bulk train from the Liverpool direction. Although it is seemingly travelling 'wrong line' on the Down Slow, the train is transferring from the Up Slow to Up Fast as it heads in the direction of Manchester. There is little mistaking that the engine is from Speke Junction with the smokebox door carrying a crudely applied 8C code - a latter day practice also shared by Patricroft. The 8F is in a deplorable condition and with steam escaping from many joints, one would assume it had little time left. However it continued in service, being transferred to Edge Hill during the following month

20th AUGUST 1967 ● N. PREEDY

The majestic lines of Royal Scot 4-6-0 No 46144 *Honourable Artillery Company* are seen to great effect in this low angle view. The engine has just crossed the Bridgewater Canal with the 1.35pm Manchester Exchange to Llandudno, and Patricroft men, Fireman Jim Carter and his driver, have put on a show for photographer Wilf Cooper in this pre-arranged photograph. The enginemen, ever eager to be caught on camera, acknowledge his presence. This 'Scot' was a regular visitor to Manchester during its spell as a Llandudno Junction engine.
1962 ● W.D. COOPER

MOTIVE POWER USED ON THE LLANDUDNO CLUB TRAIN DURING THE BR PERIOD

Llandudno Junction Shed provided the engine for the 'Club' train, which left Llandudno for Manchester Exchange with 11 coaches at 7.40am, calling at all stations to Prestatyn, then running non stop to Chester. Three cleaners were delegated each evening to prepare the engine for the following morning. After Nationalisation and throughout the 1950's, Stanier Caprotti Class Fives Nos 44738-40 monopolised the service. In 1960 they were joined by Nos 44686/7, the last pair of the class to be built, again with Caprotti valve gear and high running plates. At the end of the 1961 Summer Timetable, Class 7P engines were 'cascaded' after the introduction of English Electric Type 4 diesels on the West Coast Main line. Llandudno Junction received a number of Rebuilt Patriots, Jubilees and Royal Scots, some of which were considerably better than others. The favourite Scots were Nos 46144 *Honourable Artillery Company*, 46148 *The Manchester Regiment* and 46155 *The Lancer*. In December 1962, Britannia Pacifics Nos 70014 *Iron Duke*, 70015 *Apollo*, 70016 *Ariel* and 70033 *Charles Dickens* arrived, but could not keep time on the tightly scheduled train, owing to their poor condition through lack of regular maintenance. From January 1963, the train was regularly in the hands of one of Stanier's trusty Class Five 4-6-0's. By February, No 45311, recently ex-works, was the regular loco and was capable of running at a sustained speed of 70mph between Prestatyn and Chester. Others which featured included Nos 45149, 45282/5 and 45327. By 1965, most of the regular Manchester to North Wales trains had been dieselised with suburban DMU's, but following complaints from passengers about their riding qualities at speed, steam hauled corridor stock was re-introduced on 22nd March 1965, until diesel sets of the 'Inter-City' type (eg. what later became Classes 123/4) could be made available - which never happened! The 4.30pm from Manchester Exchange, now reduced to 7 coaches, was regularly worked by No 45285. When Llandudno Junction Shed closed on 3rd October 1966, the diagrams were transferred to Patricroft who used their better Standard Class Fives, which were Nos 73006/71 and 73137/9. Double chimney No 44766 from Chester had the honour of heading the last steam hauled 'Club' train, which ran on 30th December 1966.

On 30th October 1867, Nasmyth-Wilson and Company was formed. They began by producing machine tools and stationary steam engines at their Bridgewater Foundry and, not least, developed the steam hammer - which brought worldwide recognition to its inventor James Nasmyth. By 1882 they concentrated entirely on locomotive construction, becoming one of the foremost manufacturers in the country. The last engine to be completed was in 1938 by which time some 1,632 examples had left the works, the vast majority were for export with over half destined for the Asian market. Nasmyth-Wilson closed in 1939, at which time the premises became the property of the Ministry of Supply. After the war, ownership then passed to the M.O.D. as a Royal Ordnance Factory, but the early rail connections via Patricroft Station Goods Yard survived into the BR period. Part of the old works building, which was situated alongside the Bridgewater Canal is visible, and is now in private ownership. The original bridge which carried the Liverpool & Manchester Railway over the canal, was the subject of many early lithographs. **1960 ● SALFORD LOCAL HISTORY LIBRARY**

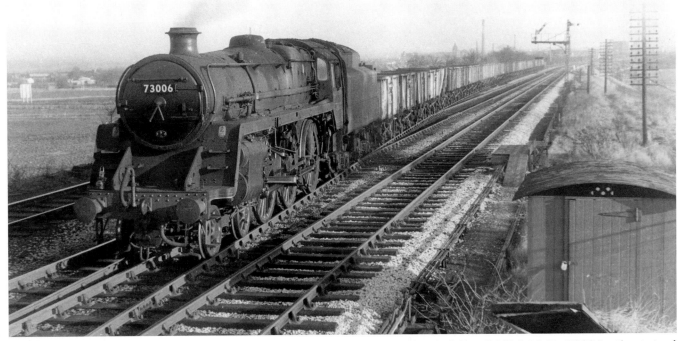

Transferring from the Down Slow to Down Fast at Barton Moss Junction is Standard Class 5 MT 4-6-0 No **73006** with a train of mineral empties. This engine enjoyed a rather chequered career. Five of the first series (Nos 73005-9) were allocated to Perth from new where they were used on trains to Inverness, Aberdeen and Glasgow. Express work included titled trains such as the *Fair Maid, Bon Accord, Granite City* and *Saint Mungo* for which they were kept in pristine condition. The loco moved on to Corkerhill, Glasgow in January 1963 before taking up residence at Patricroft 18 months later. A padlocked signal lampman's hut is evident - constructed of timber with asbestos roof. Note the ventilation holes above the door. **DECEMBER 1964 ● SALFORD LOCAL HISTORY LIBRARY**

Another member of the class, No 73069, with makeshift front numberplate, works westbound across the Barton Moss. The unstable peat moss was a considerable barrier to the builders of the Liverpool and Manchester Railway but engineer George Stephenson developed the ingenious idea of floating straw bales to gain stability for the Permanent Way formation. No 73069 was a much travelled loco, going new to Derby then to Leeds Holbeck before working out of sheds on the ex-Great Central main line. After spells at Cricklewood, Leamington Spa and Tyseley, it came north, firstly to Bolton in April 1966, then to Patricroft and finally Carnforth. It was involved in a number of enthusiasts' railtours but in May 1968 had problems with its chimney and received that from withdrawn sister engine No 73157. **JUNE 1968 ● BERNARD CRICK**

· 34 ·

PATRICROFT MPD

Francis W. Webb's reign as Chief Mechanical Engineer of the LNWR lasted from 1871 until 1903. During this period over 50 new engine sheds were constructed to the standard 'Northlight' pattern, the last of which was Patricroft (New), completed in December 1904. The ten-road building housed 50 engines, although the original plans were for more. Any extension on the eastern side of the existing building would have involved the demolition of the coal stage. The new shed, intended primarily for freight engines, was therefore built at right angles and a duplicate coaling stage was provided, again with tank over the top. It contained a wheel drop and sheerlegs, supported by a small workshop. The shed buildings and facilities, together with associated goods yards, were bound within a triangular site created by the Manchester to Liverpool main line, the Monton line and the the Patricroft Junction to Molyneux Junction branch. From this low angle view, every road appears to be occupied by a good cross-section of LNWR locomotives.   **c.1920 ● ALLAN SOMMERFIELD COLLECTION**

LNWR DAYS

A Webb 4' 3" 0-6-0 Coal Engine, No 2107 stands in the new shed yard behind which is a 'Cauliflower' 0-6-0. With the opening of this building in early 1905, the sub-shed at Ordsall Lane eventually closed and was demolished shortly afterwards. Nearly 120 locomotives were allocated to Patricroft at the Grouping, the majority of which were freight types involved in workings from a number of goods yards in the area.

c.1920 ● PAUL SHACKCLOTH COLLECTION

Renewed Precedent (or Large Jumbo) Class 2-4-0 No 2192 *Caradoc* stands by the coaling stage. This was another large class of engines designed by Webb and built between 1887 and 1901. Of the 166 built, less than half were in service at the end of the LNWR on 31st December 1922. The LMS allotted numbers 5000-5079 but 33 were withdrawn without ever acquiring them, including *Caradoc*, which was taken out of service in July 1927. Very few ex-LNWR engines survive in preservation, but a member of this class, No 790 *Hardwicke,* happily resides at the National Railway Museum at York.

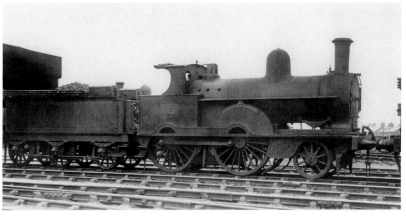

1924 ● JOHN RYAN COLLECTION

Ex-Lnwr Locos

A Superheated 'Precursor' 4-4-0, No 25272 _Brindley_ stands in the 'old' shed yard. It entered service in October 1905 as a saturated loco with slide valves, numbered 1363 and carried the name _Cornwall_. It was renamed _Brindley_ in May 1911 and seven years later entered Crewe Works to be superheated and rebuilt to piston valve in common with many others of the class. It was renumbered 5272 in August 1927 and further renumbered with the prefix '2' in October 1936, but was withdrawn just over three years later. 0-8-0 G2a Class No **8903** is behind, just within the shed building. **1937 ● PAUL SHACKCLOTH COLLECTION**

Another member of the class, No 25211 _Aurania_ stands alongside the new shed building, just off the turntable. In 1923 the LMS inherited eighty members of the class which were still running in original condition. No 5211 (LNWR No 113) was dealt with in November 1927 after which it became a Patricroft engine until withdrawal in September 1936. In 1926, the allocation of the larger ex-LNWR locomotives was as follows:

Prince of Wales 4-6-0's	5734 - 5751 (18)
George the Fifth 4-4-0's	5396 - 5403 (8)
Precursor 4-4-0's	5251 - 5259 (9)
Renown 4-4-0's	5117 - 5119 (3)
Precedent 2-4-0's	5043/5/6 (3)
Waterloo 2-4-0's	5097/8 (2)

APRIL 1936 ● W. POTTER

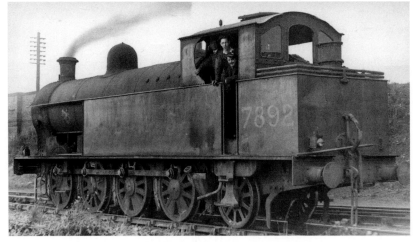

By 1933, Patricroft's allocation of 100 locos included 4 'Claughton' 4-6-0's which had been displaced elsewhere on the LNWR system. With 15 'Precursors' and 'George the Fifth' 4-4-0's and no fewer than 22 'Prince of Wales' 4-6-0's, they had an impressive array of larger engines. For more mundane work, a couple of 0-8-2 Tanks were available and regularly employed on the Manchester Docks branch between Eccles and Weaste Junction. The three figures on the footplate of No **7892** seem happy to pose for the camera. The class was introduced in 1911 and this engine was one of the last in service, being withdrawn in February 1948.

AUGUST 1946 ● W.D. COOPER

The last surviving Whale 19" Goods at Patricroft was **No 8801.** The 4-6-0 is seen basking in the Spring sunshine, six months before withdrawal in November 1948. It was one of 67 locos allocated on 1st December 1945, whose classes and numbers are as follows:

Class 3 2-6-2T: 138, 207, 209
MR Class 2P 4-4-0: 332, 507, 527, 528
LMS Class 2P 4-4-0: 628
Class 4 2-6-4T: 2454, 2560, 2561, 2573, 2574, 2596
Class 5 4-6-0: 5055, 5111, 5135, 5182, 5199, 5231*, 5259, 5290, 5304, 5315, 5329, 5377, 5386, 5397, 5401, 5402, 5408, 5420, 5421, 5424, 5426, 5428*, 5444, 5446 *Preserved*
'Patriot' Class 6P 4-6-0: 5528, 5542, 5543, 5550
Ex-LNW Class 6F 0-8-2T: 7876, 7878, 7892
Ex-LNW Class 4F 4-6-0: 8801, 28786
Ex-LNW Class 7F 0-8-0: 8903, 8912, 8920, 8941, 9095, 9199, 9254, 9255, 9273, 9304, 9330, 9353, 9405
Ex-L&Y Class 2F 0-6-0: 12019, 12030, 12031, 12036, 12049, 12059

MAY 1948 ● W.D. COOPER

One of the numerous Webb 17" Coal Class, 0-6-0 No 8288 rests in the shed yard between duties. They entered service between 1873 and 1892 and 500 were built specifically to handle coal traffic. 35 members survived Nationalisation and the last examples could be found pottering about as works shunters at Crewe. All had gone by the end of 1953.

5th MAY 1935 ● PAUL SHACKCLOTH COLLECTION

A 'Super D' 0-8-0 in LMS days. No 9218 with a tender full of coal will shortly be away from the shed fulfilling its next duty. Unusual features regarding these locomotives were the 'H' section spokes and combined sand boxes and splashers over the leading pairs of wheels.

AUGUST 1937 ● W. POTTER

Patricroft shed opened on 1st January 1885 to help ease the congestion of an ever increasing number of locomotives on the LNWR in the area. It became the premier depot and was coded '34' with both Ordsall Lane and Plodder Lane coming under its control as sub-sheds. A traditional brick-built, eight road building which could accommodate 32 locos was provided. It had a 'Northlight' roof and facilities included a standard coal stage with tank over the top. Offices and stores were situated at the rear and a 42ft turntable was installed in the yard. Much of the building was demolished early in 1938 - the reasons for which remain obscure - leaving the rearmost four roof section and the office block only. The shed was rebuilt by BR in 1956 with transverse pitched roof to a standard style. The photograph shows the original building in a rather sorry state three years before demolition. The shed roads, numbered from west to east, hold an interesting selection of locomotives. Nearest to the camera on No 3 road is Stanier Class Five No **5132**. Unrebuilt Patriot No **5516** comes next *(see below)* and just discernible within the building on No 5 road is an ex-GWR 2-6-0. Occupying No 7 road is a Precursor whilst LMS 2P 4-4-0 No **652** is on the last road, near the coal stage.   **1935 ● GORDON COLTAS**

The driver of Unrebuilt Patriot 4-6-0 No 5516 stands proudly by his engine. This side-on photograph was the next in sequence to that above and reveals yet another ex-GWR engine on shed! No 5516 was delivered new to Kentish Town on 11th October 1932 and came north to Patricroft on 20th April 1935. It wasn't at 10C long and moved again on 4th January 1936 to Camden. It was named *The Bedfordshire and Hertfordshire Regiment* on 31st July 1938 after which time it worked out of a number of sheds including Edge Hill in the 1950's, which would bring it regularly into the Manchester area on the Liverpool to Hull and Newcastle services.   **1935 ● GORDON COLTAS**

Stanier Class 4 2-6-4T No 2662 (10C) occupies No 1 road and is standing over the inspection pit that was originally within the 1885 building.

    1938 ● PAUL SHACKCLOTH COLLECTION

Both before and during World War 2, Patricroft serviced former GWR locos which worked into the Manchester area by arrangement on a daily basis. A great variety of classes appeared over the years on both passenger and freight duties into Exchange Station and Liverpool Road Goods. The shed played regular host to Moguls which monopolised the freight duties and one could usually be found on shed during the day, whilst the GWR enginemen lodged at the nearby barracks. According to records, at least one 2-8-0, No 2828 also appeared during 1933. 4-6-0 No **2922 Saint Gabriel** is one of the true 'Saints' introduced in September 1907 and built with a saturated long cone boiler and curved frame ends. They were amongst the most popular express passenger locomotives on the former GWR, designed by Churchward and had a reputation for free running. 77 engines made up the class, 14 of which were rebuilt from 4-4-2's. The 'Saint' is stabled alongside an unidentified Mogul, having worked into the city on a Saturday excursion train. The size of board on to which the reporting number 623 has been pasted is worthy of comment. The last two Moguls recorded on shed were Nos 6329/37 on 12th September 1942.   **5th SEPTEMBER 1936 ● G. HARROP**

GREAT WESTERN PRESENCE AT PATRICROFT

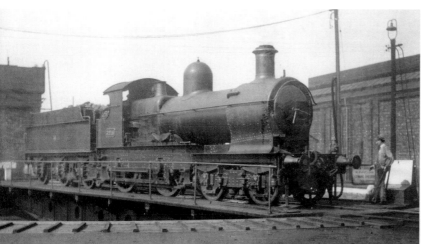

The Annual Railway Carnival held at Belle Vue brought many unusual locos into the city. A special from the Cambrian Section arrived in Manchester Exchange double headed by two ex-GWR 4-4-0's - 'Earl' Class No 3211 piloted by 'Duke' Class No 3268 *Chough*. Shortly afterwards, another double header brought in two more 'Earls', No 3212 piloting No **3216**. All four were Oswestry engines and retired to Patricroft shed for servicing. In previous years, others had been observed working throughout from Aberystswyth and Machynlleth sheds. No 3216 is accommodated on the Patricroft turntable

10th SEPTEMBER 1938 ● GORDON COLTAS

Forty members of the 'Duke' Class 4-4-0 were built between 1895 and 1899 and were the largest engines permitted over certain sections of the GWR system, which included the Cambrian. In 1946 the surviving 'Dukes' and 'Dukedog' rebuilds were renumbered in the 9000 series which allowed the Collett 0-6-0's under construction to become the 32XX series. No **3268 Chough** has an ex-LNWR 0-8-2T for company in the shed yard. The last two surviving Dukes were Nos 9084 *Isle of Jersey* and 9089 which were both withdrawn in 1951.

10th SEPTEMBER 1938 ● GORDON COLTAS

THE OLD SHED YARD

The all too familiar view from the footbridge which was the official entrance to Patricroft shed. A number of engines are present in the 'old' shed yard, including three Standard Class Fives, a Jubilee showing a reporting number and an unrebuilt Patriot. Stanier Class Five No **44905** arrives on shed whilst a Royal Scot heads a line of locomotives under the coaling plant. On 10th October 1955 heavy repairs commenced on the coaling plant under which passed two lines. Two of the four lines which offered connections between Old and New shed were 'in possession', and the other pair were constantly occupied by coal trucks and engines awaiting coaling. Facilities were normally fairly flexible and locos could enter from either direction for servicing. Similarly, engines would both arrive and depart on and off the shed in each direction at any time, necessitating both the signalboxes at Patricroft Sidings and Eccles Junction to remain open at weekends (except 6pm - midnight on Sundays). However 'one way traffic' had to be enforced with incoming engines at the Patricroft end only. Normal procedure re-commenced on 13th December 1955.   **JULY 1959 ● SALFORD LOCAL HISTORY LIBRARY**

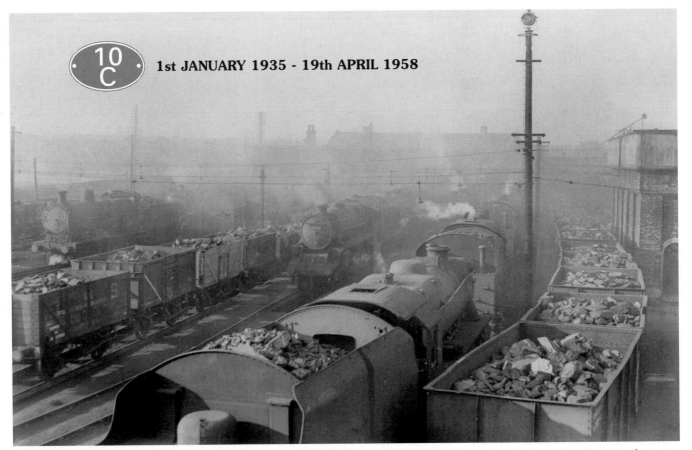

10C **1st JANUARY 1935 - 19th APRIL 1958**

A pall of smoke hangs over the old shed yard. The roof of the original LNWR building which had been in a dire state for many years, was rendered unsafe and demolished along with the rest of the building. The offices and stores at the rear survived and the roof remains in view through the murk. Accommodation in the meantime is obviously at a premium with mineral wagons containing loco coal occupying what used to be number six road.   **c1952 ● SALFORD LOCAL HISTORY LIBRARY**

INSIDE THE OLD SHED

No 40681 bathes in bright sunlight just within the shed building. This and No 40453 were Patricroft's last two ex-LMS 2P 4-4-0's, being withdrawn in August and October 1962. They were part of the shed's allocation of 72 locos on 1st January 1961 which comprised:

Class 2P 4-4-0: 40453, 40586, 40681
Class 2 2-6-2T: 41283/7
Class 4 2-6-4T: 42439/42/58/68/94, 42561/74, 42660
Class 5 4-6-0: 44708, 44808, 45095/6, 45129/33/82/95/99, 45252/5/94, 45304/52/77/8, 45409/11/20/4/42
Class 6P 4-6-0: 45558/63, 45600/45, 45663
Class 3F 0-6-0T: 47365/78, 47430/91, 47621
Class 7F 0-8-0: 49034/87, 49119/47/99, 49209, 49323/35, 49421/6
BR Class 5 4-6-0: 73030/44, 73125-34
WD Class 8F 2-8-0: 90183, 90399, 90530/68/70, 90669

1961 ● IAN COCKCROFT

A rather forlorn sight tucked away out of steam in the far corner of the shed is rebuilt Patriot 4-6-0 No **45531 *Sir Frederick Harrison.*** This locomotive had been a regular throughout the 1950's working past the shed on the Liverpool to Hull and Newcastle services, but was at Carlisle Upperby (12B) when recorded here. The shed has always been associated with the class and during the LMS period - Nos 5528/42/3/50 were at 10C during the war years and were still there in November 1945 but had moved on before Nationalisation. None were allocated in BR days but they remained regular visitors, particularly those from Carlisle Upperby whose engines regularly worked into the area.

AUGUST 1964 ● W.D. COOPER

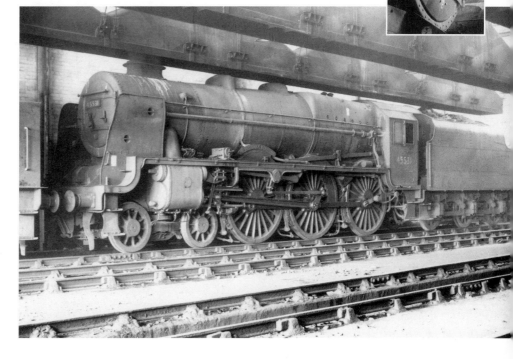

The second Standard locomotives to be introduced were the Class 5MT 4-6-0's. Like their predecessors the Britannias, the first batch were originally fitted with chime whistles immediately behind the chimney. They were subsequently removed although the Pacifics retained theirs. No **73071** is an occupant at the rear of the old shed which is in the process of receiving a new roof. In constructing the framework, BR engineers have made use of old rails as roof trusses. An archway leading to offices and stores is visible within the recently whitewashed back wall of the shed. This engine entered service at Chester in November 1954 before being sent to Kings Cross in February 1956 for exhaustive trials. It returned to Chester 15 months later and after spells further south, eventually gravitated to Patricroft. New locos Nos 73073/4 arrived here in December 1954, but the shed seemed to be temporarily out of shed plates as these two, and 'Super D' No 49034, which had recently arrived from the closed Plodder Lane, had 10C - PATRICROFT painted in white across the bottom of their smokebox doors.

1957 ● W.D. COOPER

The new shed shelters an intruder in the form of 'Crab' 2-6-0 No **42725**, in steam from nearby Bolton but formerly an Agecroft stalwart. None of this class of 245 locos, some built locally at the ex-L&Y works at Horwich - but the majority at Crewe, were ever allocated to this former LNWR stronghold - even in BR days. The stablemate is one of Patricroft's own Stanier 2-6-4 tanks, No **42442**.

1964 ● W.D. COOPER

20th APRIL 1958 - 8th SEPTEMBER 1963

THE NEW SHED

Towards the end of steam, the 'New Shed' always seemed to have an air of desolation. Some of the local spotters called it the 'dead shed' as Sunday visits often revealed only the odd loco in light steam and you could often hear a pin drop in there. Freight locos tended to monopolise the building but occasionally one of their Jubilees could be discovered, hiding away in a corner. Stanier 8F 2-8-0 No **48374** had less than a month left in service when Tom Heavyside made this Saturday visit in June 1968. The shed, now devoid of much of its roof and smoke vent panels, allows the sunlight to weave patterns along the loco's boiler.

15th JUNE 1968 ● TOM HEAVYSIDE

9th SEPTEMBER 1963 - 1st JULY 1968

The top of the ash plant was an excellent vantage point for many of Jim Carter's photographs and this one shows off the graceful lines of Rebuilt Patriot 4-6-0 No **45534 *E. Tootal Broadhurst***. The locomotive vacuum pipe is in the process of being connected to the vacuum operated motor. Notice the treadboards around the well, offering enginemen a sure footing if they have to resort to manual operation. Drivers had to know and observe the strict procedures with regards to the usage of all turntables. *(see below)*   **AUGUST 1961** ● **J.R. CARTER**

One of Chester's LMS Compounds, No 41170 takes its turn on the table, having already been coaled and watered.

27th AUGUST 1949 ● **K. FAIREY**

The 70ft turntable takes the strain of the 72 ton weight of Stanier Class Five No **45110**. This loco, destined for eventual preservation on the Severn Valley Railway, had just been allocated to nearby Bolton Shed the previous month where it remained until July 1968, moving to Lostock Hall for the last few weeks in traffic.

AUGUST 1965 ● **W.D. COOPER**

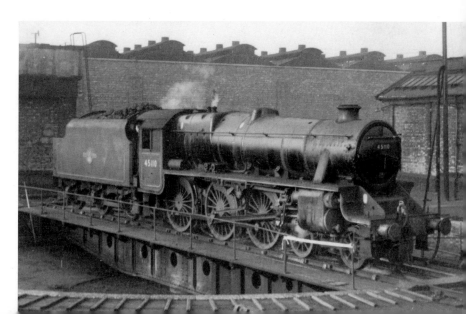

MISHAPS

Eccles Junction signalbox may be unique as the only box to be struck by not one engine, but two in separate incidents. A report on 5th September 1936 records that a light engine left the rails and crashed into the box causing considerable damage. Nearly 30 years later, Stanier Class Five No **45252** was the culprit and the box was rebuilt for a second time. As the loco is showing express passenger headlamps, the assumption is that the crew intended taking their engine to Exchange Station.

NOVEMBER 1963 ● W.D. COOPER

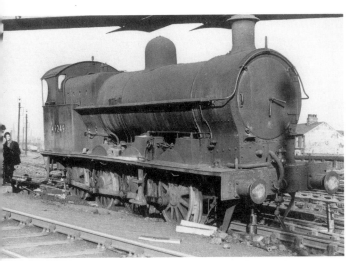

Another locomotive which has come to grief is ex-LNWR 0-8-0 No **49249,** having jumped the rails under the footbridge at the throat of the shed yard. Four months before the incident, Patricroft had been re-coded 26F after a phase of reorganisation which brought the shed under the jurisdiction of Newton Heath (26A). The breakdown train and crane from the parent depot duly arrived and re-railed the engine.

JUNE 1958 ● W.D. COOPER

A third Patricroft loco to run amok was Stanier Class Five No **45182.** Driver Frank Leater and Fireman Danny Dawson from Sutton Oak shed were the enginemen apparently responsible for this predicament. They were in the process of transferring the loco from 'old' to 'new' shed, when a misunderstanding with regards to the point setting occurred. A number of the shed's personnel are in attendance as is the Newton Heath crane once more, wedged on the table. A 'Super D' is waiting to offer assistance, ready to 'take the strain'.

1962 ● SALFORD LOCAL HISTORY LIBRARY

VISITING LOCOMOTIVES

Stanier Jubilee 4-6-0 No 45583 *Assam* had its last Heavy General Overhaul at Crewe Works between August and October 1960, during which time it received the boiler from No 45609 *Gilbert and Ellice Islands* - withdrawn in September owing to a cracked frame. This was the first 'proper' withdrawal from within the Jubilee ranks following the ill-fated No 45637 *Windward Islands* involvement in the Harrow disaster of 1952. After running-in from Crewe North, *Assam* was transferred to Llandudno Junction on 19th November 1960 and occasionally worked the 'Club' train - as on this occasion. No 45583, still in ex-works condition, drifts down the new yard prior to departure.

NOVEMBER 1960 ● J.R. CARTER

YORK

By the early 1960's, Ex-LNER visitors were becoming scarce. A Neville Hill B1 had been regularly observed in the shed yard in the mid-1950's before working the 1.25pm empty stock from Ordsall Lane to Leeds, and another, often from York, was used on the 8.25pm as well. Many others visited over the years, for example a Darlington member, No 61353 came on to the shed on 28th December 1954 having brought an excursion into Manchester. B1 4-6-0 No **61069** makes a fine sight blowing off steam before moving off shed. The engine was at York between January 1959 and September 1963.

JULY 1962 ● J.R. CARTER

LLANDUDNO JUNCTION

A regular performer on the 'Club' train during the mid-1960's was Stanier Class Five 4-6-0 No **45282**. The engine arrived at Llandudno Junction from Holyhead in February 1963 and was joined later in the year by stablemate No 45285, which came from Woodford Halse in November. This pair virtually monopolised the train for much of the period until the end of steam operation in December 1966. *(see Page 123)*

JULY 1962 ● SALFORD LOCAL HISTORY LIBRARY

135

CHESTER (MIDLAND)

LMS Compound Class 4P No 41120 stands in the shed yard, having received coal and water. The loco has also made use of the turntable and is now facing in the Chester direction ready for the return trip later in the day. In the early 1950's, both Chester and Llandudno Junction sheds had a number of these locos but they were largely displaced with the arrival of the Standard classes.

1952 ● W.D. COOPER

WILLESDEN

Rebuilt Patriot Class 7P 4-6-0 No 45529 *Stephenson* reverses off the turntable by the wall of the 'new' shed. These engines tended to concentrate on the former LNWR lines of the LM Region and were almost daily visitors here. A small number carried 10C shed plates in LMS days but, like the ex-LMS 'Compounds', Patricroft had none of its own during the BR period.

1962 ● J.R. CARTER

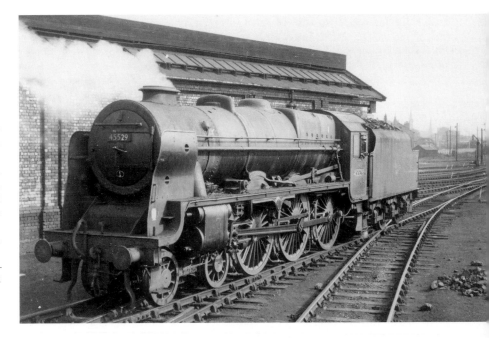

Stanier 8F 2-8-0 No 48472, a visitor from Buxton, is receiving attention in the 'new' shed yard. The Derbyshire shed had a strong association with these locos throughout the BR period but Patricroft did not receive any until the demise of the ex-LNWR 0-8-0's. In November 1962, the first 9 examples arrived and from that date until the end of steam, a steady influx came and went. No fewer than 33 were withdrawn from the shed, including 11 when it closed on 1st July 1968. The last member of the class, No 48775 moved on to Lostock Hall for a final month in service.

1965 ● SALFORD LOCAL HISTORY LIBRARY

BUXTON

WILLESDEN

Britannia Pacific No **70032** *Tennyson* moves down the 'Old' shed yard, whilst one of Patricroft's own 'Super D' 0-8-0's, No **49147** brings up the rear.

JUNE 1961 ● **J.R. CARTER**

STOCKPORT EDGELEY'S flagship engine - Fowler 2-6-4T No 42343, minus shedplate, stands amidst a number of Stanier and Standard Class Fives in the 'old' shed yard. **AUGUST 1961** ● **J.R. CARTER**

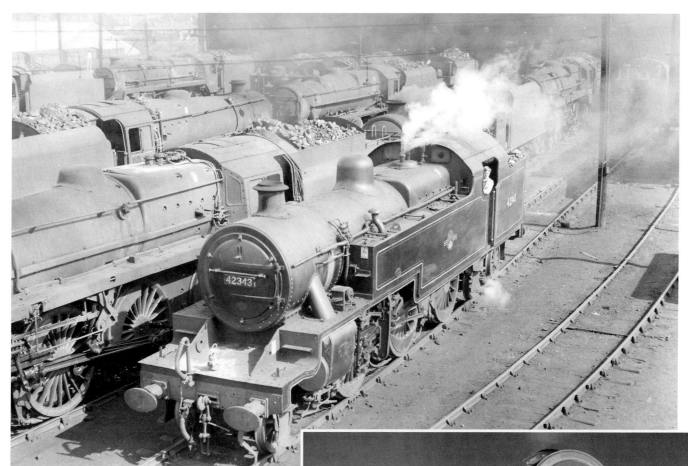

TYSELEY

BR Standard Class 9F 2-10-0 No 92223.

FEBRUARY 1966 ● **SALFORD LOCAL HISTORY LIBRARY**

CARLISLE KINGMOOR played host to the preserved Britannia Pacific No 70013 *Oliver Cromwell* in later BR days. The loco entered service in June 1951 and worked out of Norwich on the crack trains to London Liverpool Street. It arrived at Carlisle via March (31B) in December 1963 in the company of many other members of the class which had previously worked in East Anglia. It went to Upperby for a spell before returning to Kingmoor in December 1966. With the loco still in revenue earning service, this fine night portrait on the shed reveals a slight indentation in the running plate over the leading bogie wheel and that the nameplates had been removed for safe keeping by this stage. When Kingmoor Closed on 31st December 1967, *Oliver Cromwell* was transferred to Carnforth, the only 'Brit' to be allocated there, and was secured for preservation in August 1968. **APRIL 1967 ● SALFORD LOCAL HISTORY LIBRARY**

FARNLEY JUNCTION housed another high profile engine that unfortunately did not escape the cutter's torch. Jubilee 4-6-0 No **45647** *Sturdee* was one of a select band which were at this shed in early 1966. The others were Nos 45562 *Alberta* and 45581 *Bihar and Orissa,* which was withdrawn in July. Nos 45562 and 45647 moved on to nearby Holbeck in November from where they achieved fame on the *Settle and Carlisle* route and locally in the West Riding area. *Sturdee's* chimney apparently survives in a garden in the Oldham area, having been secured by Jimmy Winterbottom, a fireman at Newton Heath, who officially purchased the item by paying the princely sum of 10 shillings! **1966 ● SALFORD LOCAL HISTORY LIBRARY**

DISTINGUISHED VISITORS

CREWE (NORTH)

As a result of dieselisation of the West Coast Main Line, by mid-March 1961 only No 46209 *Princess Beatrice* of the Princess Royal Pacific Class remained in service, whilst the other eleven members were stored for the winter. No **46206 *Princess Marie Louise*,** a long standing Crewe North engine, was re-allocated to Rugby where it was stabled in a useable condition, minus its nameplates and chimney sacked over. They were re-introduced back into service at the commencement of the Summer timetable. On Saturday, 12th August, No 46206 relieved an ex-GWR Castle Class 4-6-0 loco at Shrewsbury on a Summer Saturday holiday train from the West Country. Because of ongoing electrification work, the train was diverted at Stockport and travelled via Denton and Droylsden Junctions, arriving at Manchester Victoria's No 11 platform late in the afternoon. Patricroft men were sent to relieve their Crewe North counterparts and took the empty stock to Ordsall Lane before retiring the engine to Patricroft shed. The Operating Department were most concerned on its arrival as the loco should not have traversed the viaduct straddling Irwell Street Goods Yard between Manchester Exchange and Ordsall Lane because of weight restrictions. Word quickly got around the Manchester trainspotting fraternity and Patricroft was besieged the following day. *Princess Marie Louise's* external condition was poor and many attempted to clean the cab side with handkerchiefs so as to reveal the lining. After much debate, the powers that be decided to get rid of the engine on the 1.18am newspaper train to Bangor on Monday 14th August. Patricroft men, Driver Les Pinkstone and Fireman Fred Carter took the train to Chester where they were relieved. This involved crossing the viaduct another couple of times! Also visible are three smaller Stanier locos, Nos **45390** (6J - Holyhead), **45409** (26F) and **42439** (26F).

13th AUGUST 1961 ● **J.R. CARTER**

BUXTON

An unprecedented visitor arrived one day from the Derbyshire hills. Ex-LNER J94 0-6-0T No **68006** had been kept as a spare engine at Buxton alongside No 68068 for working the northern portion of the truncated C&HP Railway, and when Patricroft needed a smaller engine to assist with shunting and shed pilot duties, the fellow ex-LNWR shed was happy to assist. The engine spent nearly six weeks at the shed before returning home and by January 1967, No 68006 was back in regular action on the Middleton Top - Friden section of the line. The white building on the left is the disposing shed whilst the sun lounger on the roof tells its own story. **FEBRUARY 1966** ● **GORDON COLTAS**

PATRICROFT'S JUBILEES

No 45668 *Madden* reverses down the yard towards the turntable. Stanier Class Fives are also in evidence and identifiable are stablemate No **45442**, awaiting its turn for coal and No **44763**, a visitor from Crewe North. An unrebuilt Royal Scot is also stabled to the left in the 'old' shed yard.   **1952 ● W.D. COOPER**

Patricroft shed has always been strongly associated with the Stanier Jubilee 4-6-0 locomotives. They were introduced into service in 1934 and members which spent periods on allocation during the LMS period included: Nos 5562/6/7/8/84/99, 5613/7/31/2/7/48/50/1/2/3, 5670/4/92, 5708/20/1/2/3/4/6. Nos 5672/89 were on loan from 5A, 30th April 1938 - 14th May 1938. Of these, two are particularly noteworthy. No 5637 *Windward Islands* was a high profile casualty of the Harrow disaster in 1952 which also involved Princess Royal Pacific No 46202 *Princess Anne*. No 5692 *Cyclops* became a Scottish loco, never to return. These Jubilees, some of which were un-named, replaced 'Claughtons' at the same time as Stanier Class Fives were replacing the 'Prince of Wales' 4-6-0's. During the early BR period, transfer activity subsided and the shed was left with six members on its books.

45558 Manitoba	December 1950 - August 1964	**45600 Bermuda**	June 1950 - January 1965
45559 British Columbia	May 1947 - November 1959	**45645 Collingwood**	September 1952 - August 1963
45563 Australia	May 1949 - September 1963	**45668 Madden**	April 1947 - October 1959

(No 45645 came from Corkerhill, Glasgow in exchange for No 45720 in September 1952. No 45668 departed for Derby in October 1959 and in return, Patricroft received No 45663 Jervis which stayed until moving to Warrington Dallam in September 1963).

The premier duty for many years was the 11.15pm newspaper train to Glasgow St Enoch, running express via Preston and Carlisle. The loco went as far as Carlisle from where it was often made use of during the day on a stopping passenger filling-in turn to Glasgow Central and return. It came home on the night fast fish from Aberdeen to Manchester Victoria. The 8.55am Newcastle to Liverpool express which was due at Manchester Exchange at 12.47pm (weekdays) was another principal turn from Leeds City. In addition to semi-fast passenger trains to Yorkshire and the North Wales coast, which they shared with Class Five motive power, they were the shed's first choice for excursion and special traffic. Many of the six enjoyed visits to London in conjunction with the Rugby League and FA Cup finals at Wembley (serviced at both Willesden and Neasden) and put in regular appearances at Scarborough during the summer months - a number of Patricroft drivers having route knowledge to the resort.

Swan song. It was perhaps fitting that the longest standing Jubilee would also be the last to depart. No **45600 Bermuda** became the 'Pride of Patricroft' and many enginemen regarded it as their finest over the years. *Bermuda* is seen here moving off shed for the last time, en-route over the city to Newton Heath shed.   **JANUARY 1965 ● SALFORD LOCAL HISTORY LIBRARY**

Jubilee 4-6-0 No 45563 *Australia* is in light steam in the 'new' shed yard. It has received the new BR number but its 3,500 gallon Fowler tender still carries the lettering LMS. Standing alongside is Caprotti Class Five No **44740** from Llandudno Junction shed which is stabled for the afternoon and will later handle the 4.30pm 'Club' train back to its home town.

12th SEPTEMBER 1950 ● H.C. CASSERLEY

No 5568 has yet to receive its name *Western Australia*. The engine was destined to spend most of its life at Leeds Holbeck, working on the Midland Main Line to London St Pancras and Bristol as well as forays over the Settle and Carlisle, and on to Glasgow. No 5568 was at Patricroft from February 1936 to May 1937 and received its nameplates on 21st September 1936.

APRIL 1936 ● W. POTTER

No 45593 *Kolhapur* became a Patricroft Jubilee for a short period between September 1964 and January 1965 at which time it left with No 45600 *Bermuda* for Newton Heath. Having spent nearly a decade at Carlisle Upperby, it made the short move to Kingmoor in September 1960 and is sporting its new 12A shedplate. Upperby engines were regular visitors to Patricroft, but No 45593 must now be classed as a stranger. The loco is one of four members now happily preserved. Another notable Jubilee that arrived from Kingmoor, via Bank Hall, in May 1964 was No 45657 *Tyrwhitt,* still bearing large cab side numbers and bracket for the tablet catcher, both a legacy of St Rollox Works. It was withdrawn four months later from Patricroft.

12th OCTOBER 1960 ● B.K.B. GREEN

In October 1962 there were five Jubilees remaining. **No 45645 *Collingwood*** and No 45558 *Manitoba* were working out mileage to secure a shopping at Crewe before next summer's service and the remaining three, Nos. 45563 *Australia*, 45600 *Bermuda* and 45663 *Jervis* were all stored in good condition (ex-works). No 45645 has the company of an unidentified Stanier 8F 2-8-0, both standing in the shed yard awaiting their next turn of duty.

6th APRIL 1955 ● GORDON COLTAS

A new class to arrive relatively late in the day were a batch of five BR Standard Class 3MT 2-6-2 Tank engines. Nos 82000/3/9/31/4 arrived from Machynlleth and Bangor (82031) sheds in March 1965. The first members of the class were introduced into service in April 1952 and, as befits locos which were both designed and built at Swindon Works, later appeared in Brunswick Green livery, fully lined out in time honoured fashion. They were still in green when they arrived at Patricroft but, for reasons of economy, the lining had been dispensed with. The forerunner of the 45 strong class, No 82000 was the exception and, other than the revised totem, is still in original condition. Sister engine No 82003, unofficially named 'Fanny', worked a 'Cotton Spinners Railtour' in the area on 16th April 1966.

1965 ● SALFORD LOCAL HISTORY LIBRARY

In 1950, the ageing Barton Wright 0-6-0's were the smallest engines available for shunting duties. To help ease the problem, Fowler 0-6-0T No 47365 arrived in September 1951 from Aston and this marked the beginning of an association with the 'Jinty' class which was to last a further 15 years. Officially 19 members were allocated at one time or another, but No **47656** was in residence during 1964/5. It was a Newton Heath engine, surplus to requirements there, which came on extended loan to help out. It was obviously a 'good un' as it carried the unofficial name **Duchess of Patricroft**, along with No 47662 which was similarly named *Tivvy*. It was common practice at many sheds to nickname their 'pet' locomotive. Stockport Edgeley, which had 'all the fours', LMS 4F 0-6-0 No 44444 at one period, christened it *City of Adswood*.

1964 ● R.S. CARPENTER

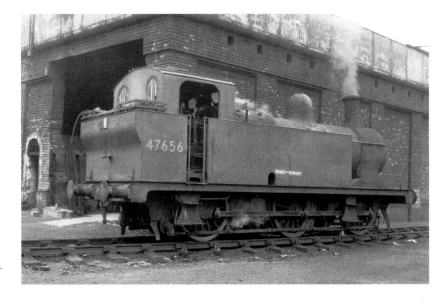

There was little in the way of local passenger work left at Patricroft when the Manchester Exchange to Wigan North Western via Tyldesley service was curtailed in April 1965. A handful of 2-6-4 tanks of both the Fairburn and Stanier variety, supplemented by Class Five 4-6-0's, had latterly shared the duties with Springs Branch shed. As they were considered unsuitable for Station Pilot duty, Patricroft disposed of its remaining ex-LMS tank engines, the last to go being No 42468 in May 1965. During the 1950's, when times were busier, long standing resident No **42561** is about to move off shed, light engine, with lamps positioned for either empty stock or a parcels train.

1956 ● W.D. COOPER

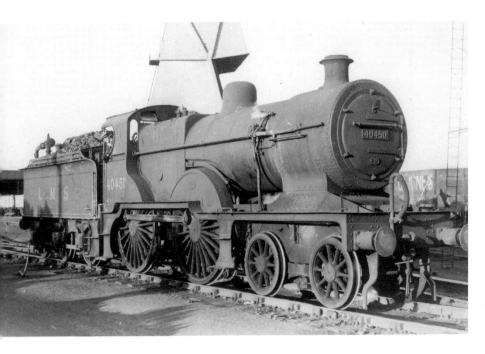

After the swift decline of ex-LNWR motive power, Patricroft had at least four ex-Midland or LMS 2P 4-4-0's to call on. The latest ex-works engine was usually employed on Exchange Station Pilot duties which also involved banking eastbound passenger trains up Miles Platting bank. Another duty was the Ordsall Lane Carriage Shed Pilot but they were regarded as 'odd job' engines and could often be found on local ballast workings. Another regular activity was trawling dead locos to Crewe Works for shopping. In 1945, Nos 332, 507, 527/8 of Midland origin and No 628 from the LMS were there, but by 1950 the older ones had been withdrawn and No 40628 had been joined by Nos 40434, **40450** and 40635. Others which arrived later were Nos 40453, 40586, 40671/6, 40681 and 40699.

1951 ● W.D. COOPER

The last surviving ex-LNWR class were the 'Super D' 0-8-0's. After Nationalisation, British Railways inherited 478 members whose numbers ranged between 48892 and 49454. The original LNWR classifications were rather complex and the engines were eventually modified into three main groups: 'G1', 'G2' & 'G2a'. No **49087** began life as a Whale Bowen Cooke two cylinder simple, non-superheated engine, being introduced in 1910, and was originally classified 'G'. It was rebuilt with a 175lb sq/in superheated boiler and Belpaire firebox which increased the tractive effort to 28,045 lb. after which the engine was re-classified 'G2a' - 7F. A low sun shows off the rugged lines of this locomotive which, despite having an uncomfortable cab layout, were renowned for being both strong running and free steaming. They lasted until the mid-1960's - which was a testament to their durability. No 49087 was withdrawn from Patricroft in September 1962.

1961 ● J.R. CARTER

The sheds at Wakefield (ex-L&Y), Springs Branch and Patricroft (ex-LNWR) were the last bastions of the Barton Wright 'Class 25' 0-6-0 locomotives which had been classified 1 and later 2F by the LMS. No **52024** is at rest between spells of shed pilot duty. In January 1952, Nos 52016/24/30/1 shared shunting duties at Cross Lane, Ordsall Lane and Liverpool Road as well as some shed pilot work. In October 1952 No 52045 arrived from Springs Branch to replace the withdrawn No 52030 and, rather surprisingly, an ex-Midland veteran 0-6-0, No 58174 arrived in place of No 52031 in February 1955 followed by two more, Nos 58279/88, which came from Walsall in March 1956. One of two survivors of a class that once numbered 50, No 52016, was regularly employed as Patricroft Station Sidings Pilot - a duty which never took it more than a 1/4 mile from the shed. It lasted until October 1956 at which time it was involved in a collision in the shed yard with a visiting WD 2-8-0. This left No 52044 at Wakefield which was secured for preservation after its withdrawal in June 1959.

12th SEPTEMBER 1950 ● H.C. CASSERLEY

In BR days, Patricroft had been closely associated with Standard Class Five 4-6-0's. Three pairs of locomotives went new to the depot from Derby Works - Nos 73023/4 in November 1951, Nos 73043/4 in October 1953 followed by Nos 73073/4 in December 1954. In addition, Nos 73090-99 arrived in late 1955. This last batch of 10 were exchanged for Caprotti examples, Nos 73125-34, from Shrewsbury (84G) in August 1958. Many others gravitated to the shed including Nos 73050 and 73096, which returned in July 1965. Both these locos happily survive in preservation. No **73039** with a typical makeshift front number-plate brews up in the 'old' shed yard. This much travelled loco had seen service at Bristol, St. Philip's Marsh, Birkenhead, Willesden, Bletchley and Nuneaton. In addition, Standard Class 4 4-6-0's from Swindon Works arrived in the shape of Nos 75010-14 in November/December 1951 before moving on to Llandudno Junction in September 1953.

APRIL 1966 ● TREVOR GRIMSHAW

Johnson 'Large Midland Tank' Class 0-6-0T No 47201 was the subject of an aborted preservation attempt by the Manchester Rail Travel Society. The engine had recently been outshopped and was considered a prime candidate - nevertheless, the 'Jinty' had been sold to Thomas Ward in Sheffield for scrap. Despite attempts to save it, BR remained adamant that the contract with Ward's was binding - Thomas Ward couldn't re-sell the locomotive and BR refused to accept it back. As a consequence, it was eventually cut up in Sheffield. No 47201 is standing stored alongside the Old shed awaiting it's fate.

DECEMBER 1966 ● BERNARD CRICK

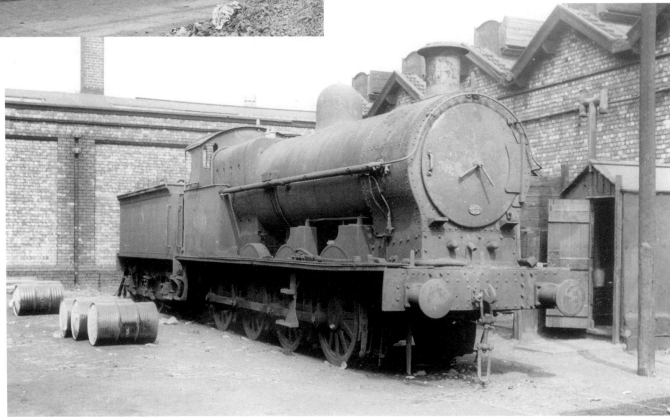

Languishing at the back of the shed buildings is ex-LNWR 'Super D' 0-8-0 No 49149. The loco looks a sorry sight with its flaking paintwork - the result of being stored in the open for over nine months whilst retaining its 26F shed plate. It was officially withdrawn in November 1959 at which time the shed still had a dozen or so examples to call on. The last survivor, a long standing resident, was No 49335, which went for scrap in October 1962. Patricroft had dispensed with its last ex-LNWR locomotive. **7th AUGUST 1960 ● GORDON COLTAS**

ENGINEMEN

Driver Wilf Thorpe and Fireman 'Little' Jackie Gleeson are caught on Station Pilot duty at Manchester Exchange. 'Gentleman Wilf', as he was known, was a popular man at Patricroft, having served at the shed for many years. When Edge Hill closed to steam on 6th May 1968, No **45156 Ayrshire Yeomanry** came on to the allocation for the last two months - during which time the loco was often to be found on this job. It was also the last engine to leave the shed under its own steam on 30th June 1968.

15th JUNE 1968 ● TOM HEAVYSIDE

Driver Tommy Jones is about to reverse on to the turntable with Standard Caprotti Class Five No **73144.** His unidentified fireman is clambering back on to the footplate, having just set the road. **18th MAY 1967 ● PAUL SHACKCLOTH COLLECTION**

Driver McDermott was an old hand who unfortunately became restricted to shed duties through failing eyesight. Here he is caught on camera, wheelbarrow in hand, in the yard between the 'new' and 'old' sheds. A Standard Caprotti Class Five stands withdrawn whilst a Class 40 diesel unit buffers up to a Stanier Class Five in the 'Old' shed yard. Main line diesels tended to congregate here and were rarely seen within the confines of the 'new' shed building. McDermott was a man often in demand by his colleagues as he was the unofficial provider of cigarettes and pipe tobacco at the shed!

12th FEBRUARY 1968 ● PAUL SHACKCLOTH

Four engines stand lifeless in the sunshine, awaiting their final trip to the scrapyard and an appointment with the cutter's torch. This unusual view is taken from the platform on the coaling stage after Patricroft had closed to steam.

22nd JULY 1968 ● BERNARD CRICK

In 1934/5, the LMS upgraded the facilities at Patricroft. A new coal plant by Messrs. Henry Lees and Company was one of the larger, No 1 variety with wagon hoist and consisted of a pair of twin bunkers, each of 75 ton capacity, which enabled different grades of coal to be delivered to the engines. In addition, a new 70ft turntable and improved ash disposal facilities were installed whilst the 'new' shed received a single pitch roof, replacing the earlier 'Northlight' pattern. For reasons unknown, the 'old' shed wasn't dealt with during this period *(see page 128)*. This view of the imposing 'coaler' has been taken from a passing train, evidently during a quiet spell, as no engines are present.

1st SEPTEMBER 1965 ● GRAHAM WHITEHEAD

In days of old, Patricroft was often a 'tough nut to crack' and many a trainspotter has trudged back across the footbridge having been ejected with only a handful of numbers scribbled in his notebook. Towards the end of steam when closure was imminent, the authorities adopted an almost cavalier attitude and trespass was a forgotten word. The 'open house' policy has apparently extended to families with young children on this occasion. Stanier Class Five 4-6-0 No **45156 *Ayrshire Yeomanry*** is the only engine in steam in the 'old' yard also occupied by a pair of English Electric Type 4s and a BR/Sulzer Bo-Bo (D5000 series) Main Line Diesel.

12th JUNE 1968 ● PAUL SHACKCLOTH

Scaffolding poles were utilised at a number of sheds after the electrification of certain lines within the former LMS network. They were used for instructional purposes as well as acting as a reminder regarding the potential hazards of working on the footplate 'under the wires'. The cross-member was set at the exact height of the catenary carrying the current. A pair of 'gauges' were erected on Patricroft's No 1 road on which an English Electric Type 4 Diesel, **D373** is standing, nosing out of the shed. The Standard Class Five is none other than No **73050**, destined for preservation on the Nene Valley Railway. 15th JUNE 1968 ● TOM HEAVYSIDE

The line from Eccles Junction to Springs Branch opened on 1st September 1864, offering a convenient route to Wigan and Preston, avoiding the Bolton district. The complexity of trackwork in the vicinity of Eccles Junction is evident in this view looking west from 'four bridges'. This was a favourite location for enthusiasts to observe traffic. Expresses coming off the Moss, hurtling through Patricroft Station at great speed before seemingly braking at the last minute were impressive, whereas westbound trains were opening out. The Engineers' Sidings are on the extreme right followed by the Down and Up main and loop lines curving away towards Monton which handled a variety of trains. With the constant movements on and off shed, there were few prolonged quiet spells. Passenger excursion stock can be seen stabled in the Down loop, which was common practice during the summer months. The engine release road from the 'new' shed yard, directly on to the Up loop, is prominent. Patricroft Sidings are situated either side of the signalbox of the same name, beyond which are the Up and Down slow and fast lines to Chat Moss and beyond.

JULY 1959 ● SALFORD LOCAL HISTORY LIBRARY

THE MONTON LINE

Attacking the Monton curve is Unrebuilt Patriot 4-6-0 No **45524** *Blackpool* from Carlisle Upperby (12A) with a northbound express passenger train. The Engineers' Sidings feature this time on the left, part of which formed the short-lived curve (1884-1891) which once offered a connection from Eccles Junction to the Clifton branch. Patricroft North Sidings, situated behind the 'old' shed and alongside the 'new', are out of view on the right. Incidentally, the Patriots were referred to as 'Chinese Compounds' by the older Patricroft enginemen.

1951 ● SALFORD LOCAL HISTORY LIBRARY

A trio of locos at work. Jubilee 4-6-0 No **45635** *Tobago* takes the Monton line at Eccles Junction with the afternoon Barrow train whilst Caprotti Class Five No **44738** from Llandudno Junction shed (6G) drifts off shed light engine, prior to working the Llandudno 'Club' train. Barton Wright 0-6-0 No **52045** is engaged on shed pilot duty. *Tobago* appears to have a scorched smoke-box door - an unusual sight on a Jubilee which would soon be attended to at Newton Heath. The wooden post signal in view is in the process of being replaced by its tubular steel counterpart, which awaits the fitment of arms and signal lamps before being ready for commission.

1954 ● **W.D. COOPER**

Regular performers on the Monton line were the Riddles designed Austerity Class WD 2-8-0 locomotives. No **90292**, working tender first towards Eccles Junction, has an interesting history. It was based on the Western Region until 1950 at which time it came north to Wakefield. In June 1956 it moved into the Manchester area working out of Agecroft shed for 7 years. A further transfer to the east side of the city at Gorton was followed be a final move to Langwith Junction in September 1964. It was withdrawn in October 1965.

1960 ● **W.D. COOPER**

An Officers' Special Train traverses the Monton line with Ivatt Mogul No **46437** in charge. This loco, which was regularly entrusted to this duty, was kept in excellent condition at Newton Heath. The 'Sectional Appendix' states that trains which comprised an engine and saloon only and run for rail officers, were not accompanied by a guard. It became the responsibility of drivers and firemen to carry out the Rules and Regulations as applicable to men in charge of a light engine. In addition, Driver 'Slow Line' Jones from Newton Heath (who is working on the fast line on this occasion) would be made aware that a part of his extra duties was to check couplings, brake and vacuum pipe prior to departure.

1965 ● **SALFORD LOCAL HISTORY LIBRARY**

The 4.15pm Manchester to Glasgow train travelled by way of the ex-LNWR line to Springs Branch Junction, calling at Wigan before Preston, where the Liverpool portion would be added. Polmadie 'Clan' Pacific No **72001 *Clan Cameron*** passes a mixed goods train on the Down Monton Loop with six coaches in tow, including a restaurant car, on this first stage of its journey. The coal has been carefully trimmed but the loco will undoubtedly require assistance on the climb to Shap Summit. A dirty chimney almost obliterates a Salford Corporation bus making its way down Wellington Road towards Eccles Station. **JUNE 1961 ● J.R. CARTER**

Farnley Junction Jubilees had been a common sight passing through the Patricroft area for many years and shared the principal duties between Leeds City and Liverpool Lime Street with engines from Edge Hill and Patricroft. After dieselisation of the services in 1961, they remained at the Leeds depot but were used for many secondary duties. On Summer Saturdays, as late as 1966, one was regularly entrusted with the Leeds to Llandudno train which travelled by way of Stockport Edgeley. The loco then lay over for a week before returning home the following Saturday. They also retained a presence in this area and one could regularly be seen heading a short parcels train on the Monton line towards Wigan. No **45695 *Minotaur*** is captured in presentable condition and about to pass under the Patricroft Junction to Molyneux Junction 'Black Harry' line with the working. **1964 ● W.D. COOPER**

GREEN LANE

This view will strike a chord with the many enthusiasts who travelled out of the City by bus intending to 'bunk' Patricroft shed. The corner of Green Lane and Liverpool Road was the alighting point and a short walk to Hampden Grove brought you to the shed entrance. It was then a case of ignoring the prominent official trespass sign at the footbridge entrance before crossing, always with a degree of trepidation. The majority of Sunday visitors met little resistance but weekdays were a different matter and instant ejection, coupled with threats of police action was often the case. The majority respected this and confined their unofficial visits to the day of the Sabbath when there were always more locos on shed anyway. The following extract from the gricers 'bible of the day', The *British Locomotive Shed Directory* by Aidan L. F. Fuller makes interesting reading. 'This shed is in the fork of the Eccles - Patricroft and Eccles - Monton lines. The yard is partially visible from both lines. Turn left outside Patricroft Station along a narrow road running parallel to the railway and continue into Hampden Grove. A footbridge leads from the left hand side of this road to the shed. Walking time 5 minutes. It then goes on to stress 'In no way does this book grant permission to enter any shed'. The Manchester bound buses in view are Lancashire United Transport's No **270**, a Guy Arab V with Northern Counties body on Service 45 from Hollins Green. The 6LW engine was produced locally by Gardners of Patricroft. Salford City Transport's No **183** brings up the rear on Service 67 from Peel Green (Brookhouse Estate).

7th JUNE 1969 ● P.J. THOMPSON

GARDNER & SONS LTD.

The family concern of L. Gardner and Sons Ltd, established in 1868 and based at Patricroft, had a great impact on road transport in this country which many feel has never been properly acknowledged. The legendary 6LW Gardner diesel engine, originally developed in 1931, had changed little and was in great demand by municipal and independent bus undertakings alike. It was installed in a great number of buses in the mid 1960's but the labour force had almost tripled in the early 1930's, becoming the largest employer in the Eccles area, as the Company cornered a large slice of the emerging market and went on to prosper after the war. Staunch family traditions, however, contributed towards its eventual downfall. Hugh Gardner - a third generation family member who went on to become chairman in 1955, was primarily responsible for developing the highly successful 6LX engine in 1958. Whilst charging a premium for engines that were often in short supply, he also steadfastly refused to consider turbocharging them. The business took a down turn and was eventually sold to Hawker Siddeley in 1977. They tried in vain to arrest the falling market share but sold on again. Suffice to say that current owners The Texas Group no longer manufacture or recondition Gardner engines. One of the Demonstrator Wagons, **DLG 489,** whose livery has been finished to coachwork standards, is displaying samples of the company's product.

1950 ● A. HAYNES COLLECTION

PATRICROFT JUNCTION - CLIFTON JUNCTION

THE 'BLACK HARRY' LINE

An Astley Green to Outwood loaded mineral train swings away from the main line at Patricroft Junction behind a Fowler 'Austin 7' 0-8-0 No **49667** from Bury. The branch opened in 1850 and offered a connection to Bury and beyond via the East Lancs Railway. A local passenger service was soon abandoned and the line saw little traffic over the years. Before the Second World War, Summer Saturday excursions occasionally traversed the route with trains from Lancashire to North Wales.

30th JUNE 1952 ● W.D. COOPER

The line closed completely on 28th April 1953 when Clifton Hall Tunnel collapsed and several houses fell victim in the process, killing five occupants. Afterwards, it was intended to infill the tunnel with old ballast rather than earth and to assist with the work, Departmental Diesel locomotive ED1 was sent to Patricroft on 6th April 1955, marshalled in a train with the coupling rods off. Despite the rods being refitted, it never moved - the delay presumably being caused by the lack of spent ballast. During the war, the tunnel was used by the makers of Exide Batteries, whose works were at nearby Clifton Junction, as a bomb-proof shelter for the storage of acid tanks. 'Super D' 0-8-0 No **49087** is on the truncated line, about to set back wagons into Patricroft Station Sidings.

31st MARCH 1957 ● K. FAIREY

Another 'Austin 7' from Bury, No 49508 makes a dramatic entrance from Clifton Hall Tunnel with a northbound mineral train. The principal traffic on the line came from three local collieries, Wet Earth, Clifton Hall and Wheatsheaf, with much of the coal going to Patricroft for onward transmission. **26th JANUARY 1952 ● ALLAN SOMMERFIELD COLLECTION**

Stanier Class Five 4-6-0 No 45311 (5A - Crewe North) is leaving the Monton Loop with empty stock for Oxenholme. The over-bridge in the background carried the ill-fated Patricroft Junction - Clifton Junction (Black Harry) line. **JULY 1961 ● J.R. CARTER**

The view from the overbridge looking in the Monton direction. Another Class Five, Patricroft's No **45411** approaches Eccles Junction on the Up Loop with a mixed freight from Leigh. **JUNE 1962 ● J.R. CARTER**

At first glance, one could perhaps be forgiven for believing that Daimler CVG6 No **549** had broken down en-route and was awaiting attention. However the reason is that the bus is making use of the Bluebell Hotel car park on Rocky Lane as a temporary turn back. Whitsun Anniversary processions prevented further progress along Parrin Lane to Winton and Peel Green and buses on the 66 route were using this facility until the roads cleared. No 549 was one of Salford's first batch of 8ft wide buses and until the majority of the fleet were of similar width, they carried a small red dome situated at the bottom of the front upper-saloon window pillar for the benefit of the bus wash operators at Frederick Road and Weaste garages.

1950 ● A. HAYNES COLLECTION

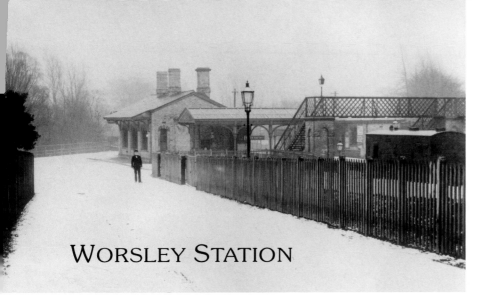

WORSLEY STATION

This Edwardian view of Worsley Station has an almost Christmas Card quality about it. A covering of snow hides the cobbled approach from Worsley Road whilst the solitary figure, who has ventured out into the cold, is possibly a railway official made aware of the impending photograph. The main building on the Up platform was a fine example of LNWR architecture. The facilities included 1st and 2nd Class waiting rooms which were also duplicated on the Down side, originally reached by means of a boarded crossing at the west end of the platforms. A horsebox stands in the dock which was used to transport stock to and from the nearby Earl of Ellesmere's estate.

c.1900 ● JOHN RYAN COLLECTION

By 1964, the horse traffic was no more. A small signalbox which stood opposite had also disappeared as well as the trailing crossover, which offered a connection to the dock. The main building, which is now devoid of its original ridged, glazed canopy, exposes the original white brickwork which had badly tarnished over the years. The original canopy on the Down platform remains in-situ and one of a similar size was all that now protected the Manchester commuter. Stanier Class Five No **45326** passes through the station and under the attractive lattice footbridge with the 9.40am Morecambe to Manchester Victoria express. **27th JUNE 1964** ● A.C. GILBERT

In 1949, Plodder Lane - the Bolton shed of the LNWR - took delivery of a batch of new Ivatt 2-6-2 tanks which replaced the old 'Coal Tanks' at a stroke. A recently delivered example, No **41215**, carrying the short lived BRITISH RAILWAYS lettering on the tank sides, awaits departure with the two coach push and pull service which operated between Bolton Great Moor Street & Manchester Exchange. The station canopy roof, referred to above, looks to be in a poor state of disrepair and may have been demolished shortly afterwards.

1949 ● W.D. COOPER

SANDERSONS SIDINGS

The 7.05pm Manchester Liverpool Road to Carlisle fast freight passes Sandersons Sidings, situated within Worsley Woods, south of Roe Green Junction. The train was diagrammed for a loco from Carlisle Upperby (12A), which has provided a Class Five 4-6-0 No **5296**, still carrying its LMS number, instead of the usual unrebuilt Patriot. Another Stanier engine waits to follow in its path with coal traffic from the interchange sidings, which offered a connection between the Bridgewater Collieries network and the LNWR.

1950 ● W.D. COOPER

After a spell of shunting, ex-LNWR 'Super D' 0-8-0 No **9134** has clear signals from Sandersons Sidings signalbox to get its train of 56 wagons underway in the Salford direction. Although the engine was locally based, carrying a 10D, Plodder Lane shedplate, an interesting allocation history followed. In 1945 it had been at the parent depot, Springs Branch (10A), but by August 1950 it had moved on to Preston (10B). After a lengthy spell at Speke Junction (8C) during the 1950's, it was again on its travels to Nuneaton (2B) in November 1959, but not before another short spell at 10A. After a two year stint in the Midlands, it ended up down the line at Patricroft from where it was withdrawn in April 1962. The bridge on which the coal wagons can be seen carries part of the mineral railway which connects Sandhole Colliery in the north with Sandersons Sidings, which were gained from a spur just beyond the bridge to the south.

APRIL 1948 ● W.D. COOPER

Carrying the later, simplified livery of a single primrose band, No **150** was one of Salford's first two Leyland Atlanteans, introduced in 1962, the other being No 149. Bodies were by Metro-Cammell. Unlike many of this type found on other systems, Salford City Transport's buses were always conductor-operated prior to the SELNEC regime. The Operating Department had a habit of 'showing off' their new vehicles in the first instance on Service 15 - which ran from Piccadilly to Worsley - so they would be noticed from the Manchester Corporation Transport Department's office windows at 55 Piccadilly. Civic pride indeed! No 150 is standing at the Worsley terminus, near the Courthouse - a local landmark in the area. Another kind of pride was at stake in May 1968 when the Queen visited Worsley to inspect 'Operation Spring Clean', a local initiative.

1962 ● J. FOZARD

With the Roe Green Splitting Distant Signal in its favour, one of the Newton Heath stud of Jubilee 4-6-0's, No **45702 *Colossus*** appears in charge of the 4.15pm restaurant car train to Glasgow Central. The immaculate loco is on the approach to Roe Green Junction and is paired with one of the smaller 3,500 gallon Fowler tenders for the long journey. The coal has had to be carefully trimmed at the shed beforehand. The train travelled over ex-LNWR metals to reach Springs Branch Junction before arriving at Wigan North Western - its first stop. This was a lodging turn to Polmadie for the men who returned with the engine on the next day's 10.40am from Glasgow Central.

APRIL 1951 ● W.D. COOPER

The 9.10am Chester to Manchester Exchange travelled by way of Tyldesley before running non-stop to Eccles. This is the same location as *Colossus,* but looking in the westerly direction towards Roe Green Junction. One of the Llandudno Junction Class 4P 4-4-0 'Compounds', No **925** is in charge of the train, due to arrive in the city at 10.48am.

1947 ● W.D. COOPER

Approaching Roe Green Junction on the Up line from the Bolton direction is Fowler Class 3MT 2-6-2T **No 58.** The light engine, running bunker first down the incline, is about to pass under Greenleach Lane bridge.

1946 ● W.D. COOPER

Crawling around the curve from Roe Green Junction and on to the Ellenbrook line is Stanier Class Five 4-6-0 No **5249**. This photograph, taken in wartime, depicts a typically grubby engine and the pall of smoke indicates that the fireman has filled the firebox. The tender has just passed over a boarded crossing which was a public 'right of way' over the railway. A trespass sign is sited at the foot of the embankment beyond which is an original LNWR lower quadrant signal. Just visible in the distance near Greenleach Lane Bridge are two tall posts, both with repeater arms, which are the Up Home Junction signals protecting the Bolton and Ellenbrook lines.

1940-45 ● W.D. COOPER

An example of Class 7 power being relegated to secondary duties. Royal Scot 4-6-0 **No 46113 Cameronian** (56D - Mirfield) is heading towards Wigan with a fitted freight which consists mainly of vans. The loco was rebuilt in 1951 and spent the rest of its life working out of Yorkshire depots. It was one of a number allocated to Leeds Holbeck which were displaced in September 1961 by the arrival of ex-LNER A3 Pacifics from Gateshead and Heaton. Three members, Nos 46113, 46117 *Welsh Guardsman* and 46145 *The Duke of Wellington's Regiment (West Riding)* went firstly to Low Moor then on to Mirfield in January 1962. Five months later they returned to Holbeck at the start of the Summer timetable for a final fling, together with Nos 46109 *Royal Engineer* and 46130 *The West Yorkshire Regiment,* which had remained at Low Moor in the meantime. All five were withdrawn in January 1963 and stored at Leeds Neville Hill for a number of months before being cut up at Crewe later in the year.

APRIL 1962 ● IAN COCKCROFT

The kind of motive power more usually associated with Mirfield shed is represented here by a grimy Austerity 2-8-0 **No 90622.** Another train of vans is travelling towards Wigan but the headlamps indicate it to be one of the loose coupled variety.

MARCH 1962 ● **IAN COCKCROFT**

The sylvan surroundings of Ellenbrook provide the perfect backdrop for a Duchess Pacific in full cry. One of Stanier's masterpiece locomotives, Class 8P No **46238** *City of Carlisle* pounds up the bank with a diverted extra working showing Reporting Number 1S90. The maroon liveried engine was by this time carrying the simplified lining applied at Crewe from January 1960. No 46238 was a Carlisle Upperby engine and if the driver was an Upperby man, he may well have the necessary route knowledge over this section as the depot had regular workings into the Manchester area. The leading two coaches are an ex-LMS articulated set originally built for the 'Coronation Scot'.

APRIL 1962 ● IAN COCKCROFT

A rare view of a Webb 'Coal' tank, No 7799 working bunker first, providing interesting detail for railway modellers. Ellenbrook Station is visible away in the distance whilst the spur to the left forming Ellenbrook Junction, connects with the extensive mineral railway system serving a multitude of collieries in the area. The loco, a resident of 10D, Plodder Lane at this time, has an interesting history. It was numbered 1054 in LNWR days, and became No 58926 during the BR era. After working on the ex-LNW lines in South Wales, it was withdrawn in October 1958 and has been preserved, currently residing on the *Keighley and Worth Valley Railway* in Yorkshire.

OCTOBER 1947 ● W.D. COOPER

Engineering work on the West Coast main line north of Crewe often resulted in many of the express trains taking the standard diversionary route via Manchester. Camden based English Electric Type 4 diesel No **D374** brings the northbound *Royal Scot* towards Ellenbrook, having already passed through Manchester and Salford. A nice feature was the retention of the distinctive tartan headboard featuring a Scottish lion on a yellow shield above the title on a Royal Stuart background. This had been worn previously by Duchess Pacifics (and others) after its inception in June 1950.   **1961 ● IAN COCKCROFT**

A grimy unidentified Stanier 8F 2-8-0 trundles down the hill from the Ellenbrook direction towards Roe Green Junction. The short coal train consists of the standard variety of BR mineral wagon but one or two wooden bodied examples are present. About 1/2 mile further on, the line passed beneath the East Lancashire Road before heading for Worsley and Eccles. Note the vandalised spectacle plate of the distant signal with repeater arm.   **1960 ● IAN COCKCROFT**

No 46257 *City Of Salford*

A BRIEF HISTORY

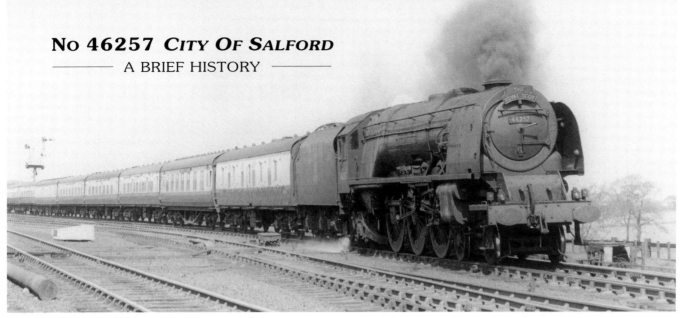

City of Salford was the last of the Stanier LMS Pacifics as part of Lot No 184, the order for two locos being placed in 1945. The last two engines were delayed because of design changes by H.A. Ivatt. Nos 6256/7 were fitted with Delta-type trailing trucks, electric lighting, modified boiler proportions, roller bearings and reversing gear - 100,000 miles a year was the target. The cab side sheets were also reduced in depth. *City of Salford* was never owned by the LMSR as it did not emerge from Crewe until May 1948. The naming ceremony took place at Manchester Exchange Station on June 3rd 1948 where Mr. R.O. Bannister, Divisional Operating Manager of the LMR (Manchester) of BR received the Lord Mayor of Salford, Alderman J. Brentnall. The policy of the railways was to name its most important engines after famous regiments, men and cities. Salford, historically, had been closely identified with railways and Mr. Bannister hoped the loco would carry the name with dignity and honour. It was turned out in the 1946 LMS livery, lined in maroon and straw as 6257M *(M underneath number)* but was renumbered 46257 before entering service at Camden shed. It stayed at Camden until January 1956 during which time it was repainted in Brunswick Green in April 1953. Along with Princess Royals Nos 46207/10 and sister No 46254, it was then temporarily transferred to Old Oak Common on the Western Region whilst a number of Kings were in Swindon Works receiving bogie modifications. It worked the Wolverhampton, Bristol and West of England services before returning to Camden at the end of February 1956. The loco was again repainted BR Standard Green in January 1958 with new tender emblem but later that year in September was transferred to Carlisle Upperby. It moved on to Kingmoor in March 1961 and was officially withdrawn from there on 12th September 1964. The loco had latterly carried the yellow diagonal stripe on the cab sides banning it from the old stamping ground under the wires south of Crewe. On 31st December 1959, the total mileage was 806,708 - considerably less than the other members of the class at the time. Unfortunately, official records ceased to be kept for the locomotive after this date. No 46257 was sold to Arnott Young, West of Scotland Shipbreaking Company, Troon, Ayrshire in November 1964, arriving there on 2nd December. Salford City Council have one nameplate whilst the other is in private ownership. 46257 is seen hauling the Up 'Royal Scot' in 1953.   **1953 ● PAUL SHACKCLOTH COLLECTION**

The engine passed through Salford on at least one occasion whilst in revenue earning service on BR. Early in 1962, a Glasgow Central to London Euston express was diverted due to engineering works. Passed Fireman Jim Carter from Patricroft was sent to Wigan North Western as passenger to pilot the loco as far as Manchester Piccadilly. When Jim stepped on to No **46257's** footplate, the driver immediately retired into the train and his fireman, although many years Jim's senior, had no route knowledge beyond Springs Branch Junction. Jim relished the challenge of driving his favourite class of loco and although the undulating road was subject to speed restrictions, he opened her up sufficiently to gather a full tender of water on Eccles Troughs. One of the last occasions the engine was in steam is captured here. **City of Salford** is standing in the west yard of Newton Heath shed prior to a nostalgic return to Manchester Exchange Station. The occasion was the crowning of the Railway Queen, Norma Corrigan, which took place on the footplate - the cab roof having received a coat of white paint for the occasion. Chalked on the cab doors is a warning, 'keep off - wet paint'. After the ceremony, the loco was observed on Springs Branch, Wigan on 11th September making its way to Preston, where it was stored in the open at the rear of the old shed, awaiting its final journey to Troon.   **SEPTEMBER 1964 ● GEORGE BINGHAM COLLECTION**

One of Edge Hill's finest. Rebuilt Patriot Class 4-6-0 No **45535 *Sir Herbert Walker K.C.B.*** heads out over Chat Moss with a Liverpool train. Herbert Walker joined the LNWR at age 17, rising to become Outdoor Goods Manager, Southern Division. He then became the General Manager of the LSWR in 1912, and of the Southern Railway in 1923. He was knighted in 1917 and is best known for his work in the south, in promoting suburban and main line electrification, development of Southampton Docks, Pullman trains and fixed interval (clock face) train departures. The building on the extreme right is the Bridgewater Hospital, immediately west of the canal. There could surely be no better place to convalesce than the upper balcony, which offered a grandstand view of the main line. **1956 ● W.D. COOPER**

The view is at Stockport Edgeley and therefore should not, strictly speaking, be included in this volume. It is full of interest, however, and has strong Salford connections. LNWR 0-8-0 No **2246** is a Patricroft engine whilst the train is one of locomotive parts, packed for shipment to the Uganda Railway from the works of Nasmyth Wilson, Patricroft. Of further interest is the LNW bracket signal protecting the scissors crossing between the Up Slow/Platform 1 line and the Up Main. A similar arrangement existed on the Down side of the station involving Platform 4. The shunting signals adjacent to the engine cab are the original LNW rotating disc pattern of 1881. The prominent overhead cables offered a connection from the main telegraph pole route to the Telegraph Office on the Up Platforms. The cabin to the right was of standard LNW design for use as mess rooms, stores and offices. In this case it was used by shunters in the adjacent coal yard and Vernon Sidings. Very few grounded vintage coach bodies, which were common elsewhere, could be found on the ex-LNWR system in later years. **1914 ● R.S. CARPENTER**

SALFORD IN THE DAYS OF STEAM

FRONT COVER. **Salford's strong association with railways in the days of steam** is epitomised in this view looking north west at Brindle Heath, which also typically reflects the cities rich industrial heritage. A signalman at Brindle Heath Junction box observes the passage of ex-WD 2-8-0 No **90292** as it coasts down the 1 in 88/132 Pendlebury incline on the slow line with a train of coal. The engine was one of 533 purchased by British Railways in October 1948, by which time it was already on loan to the Western Region, running out of Bristol, St. Philip's Marsh shed. Behind the signalbox are glimpses of Agecroft Motive Power Depot, always known simply as Agecroft engine shed in L&Y days. The four cooling towers are part of the power station complex situated between the railway and the River Irwell, adjacent to which stood the local colliery, re-opened and modernised during the early BR period. Brindle Heath Up Sidings are also in view to the right of the connecting line between here and Agecroft Junction. **4th AUGUST 1961 ● W.D. COOPER**

BACK COVER. **Hughes 'Dreadnought'** 4-6-0 No **1509**. Agecroft Shed. **c.1920 ● REAL PHOTOS**

Aspinall 'Pug' 0-4-0 Saddle Tank No **51237**. Irwell Street Goods. **18th JANUARY 1962 ● R.S. GREENWOOD**

Salford Corporation Daimler No **508** (FRJ 508). Victoria Bus Station. **1964 ● D. YOUNG COLLECTION**

Jubilee 4-6-0 No **5678 *De Robeck*.** Manchester Exchange Station. **20th MARCH 1948 ● A. HAYNES**

Stanier Class 4 2-6-4T No **42494**. Clifton Junction. **1st JUNE 1963 ● A.C. GILBERT**

Jubilee 4-6-0 No **45698 *Mars*.** Ordsall Lane. **24th MARCH 1965 ● GRAHAM WHITEHEAD**

Problem 2-2-2 No **3020 *Cornwall****. **Preserved - NRM, York* Ordsall Lane. **c.1890 ● PAUL SHACKCLOTH COLLECTION**